"Karstein Bjastad has written a superb primer for those inter-
ested in exploring the profound spiritual psychology *A Course in
Miracles* that includes an excellent summary of its underlying
metaphysics along with examples of practical applications that
will pique the interest of any sincere seeker of non-dualistic
truth. *The Naked Truth: Seven Keys for Experiencing Who You Are*
also introduces the unique forgiveness at the Course's heart, a
practice that heals our split mind, ultimately freeing us from the
imprisonment of our dream of separation from our source and
each other. I highly recommend it."
**Susan Dugan, author of *Extraordinary Ordinary Forgiveness*
and the ACIM blog**

"Karstein's great desire is to help readers understand and
negotiate the complexities of *A Course in Miracles*. The sincerity
of his effort shines through in every page of this book."
**Carrie Triffet, author of *Long Time No See* and *The
Enlightenment Project***

"True forgiveness is crucial for our peace of mind and there
cannot be too many encouraging ways to be reminded of its
importance. Take to heart Karstein's easy-to-read helpful hints
and enjoy the loving and timeless fruits of your practice."
**Carol Howe, author of *Never Forget To Laugh: Personal
Recollections of Bill Thetford, Co-Scribe of A Course in Miracles***

"I loved *The Naked Truth*. Karstein has written a clear and
practical guide to walking the spiritual path with *A Course in
Miracles*: staying true to the metaphysics of the Course while

being firmly anchored in his personal experiences. It is an enlightened read for anybody new to spirituality and is a wonderful reminder for those of us who have been on the journey for many years!"

Kenneth Bok, creator of ACIMExplained.com

"The Naked Truth presents a lucid exploration of non-dual metaphysics in a clearly written, easy-to-understand format. It is an excellent introduction to the subject on its own merits as well as a complementary resource for students of *A Course in Miracles* (ACIM). I particularly like how commonly confused ideas are brought into focus, corrected and simplified. The seven Keys are a helpful tool to assist in undoing our investment in a thought system that is a needless nightmare, when a happier dream awaits us as our birthright. I recommend this book to any student of ACIM."

Bruce Rawles, author of *The Geometry Code: Universal Symbolic Mirrors of Natural Laws Within Us; Friendly Reminders of Inclusion to Forgive the Dreamer of Separation*

The Naked Truth

Seven Keys for Experiencing
Who You Are
A Practical Guide

"Non-dualistic spirituality demystified"

The Naked Truth

Seven Keys for Experiencing
Who You Are
A Practical Guide

"Non-dualistic spirituality demystified"

Karstein Bjastad

BOOKS

Winchester, UK
Washington, USA

First published by O-Books, 2013
O-Books is an imprint of John Hunt Publishing Ltd., Laurel House, Station Approach,
Alresford, Hants, SO24 9JH, UK
office1@jhpbooks.net
www.johnhuntpublishing.com

For distributor details and how to order please visit the 'Ordering' section on our website.

Text copyright: Karstein Bjastad 2013

ISBN: 978 1 78279 087 7

A CIP catalogue record for this book is available from the British Library.

Design: Stuart Davies

Printed in the USA by Edwards Brothers Malloy

We operate a distinctive and ethical publishing philosophy in all
areas of our business, from our global network of authors to
production and worldwide distribution.

CONTENTS

This book is lovingly dedicated to my wife Lucy Johnson and to Gary R. Renard, who has opened my, my wife's and so many other people's eyes to a wondrous journey and its glorious destination.

Preface

In the Preface 2004 of the 25th anniversary edition of his book *Love is Letting Go of Fear*, Gerald G Jampolsky shares that he is dyslexic, and that one of his college professors told him never to try to write a book.

I remember at times during my junior high years thinking what an achievement it was to write a book. That writing a book was an achievement beyond anything I could ever hope to accomplish, as though at some level I was tuning into the idea of wanting to write a book. My reality at that time though was that I struggled to read a novel while at the same time comprehend the story, since I dispensed so much of my mental effort on merely reading the words. So the thought of *writing* a book seemed like fantasy.

Ten to fifteen years ago, now well into my working years and with both a graduate and a post-graduate degree behind me, I remember the thought surfacing again about writing a book. My sense was that it was going to be a book about how to live a better life, with a somewhat ethical bias. This was before spirituality had entered my life in a big way. So within my conceptual mindset at the time this was how I was able to interpret the thoughts that surfaced.

Reading the Preface 2004 of *Love is Letting Go of Fear* helped me become more confident that I could write a book. As my understanding of non-dualistic spirituality developed, it gradually became clear to me what book I was meant to write; a book I seemingly connected with all the way back in junior high. You are now holding that book in your hands.

A concept mentioned in a number of spiritual texts is that you should teach what you want to learn. What this book is about is what I want to learn. And it is a book I wish was available in the earlier part of my spiritual studies and practice.

This book is short, comprehensive, to the point and practical.

One of the pre-requisites for achieving the aim of this book, the experience of who you are, is to first experience peace of mind. Peace of mind is a by-product of the spiritual practice this book introduces you to.

While earlier I viewed my less than average reading ability as a hindrance, I am now at peace with it. I realize that if I were to need better reading abilities in order to achieve my goal, my reading abilities would have been better. All is as it should be. Through the application of the Keys presented in this book, I am achieving newfound peace of mind in connection with other aspects of my life too.

For me this journey is still ongoing. Thanks to the loving nature of the Keys, the ongoing journey largely unfolds with grace. For the rest of my journey I would love to have you join me; join me towards our goal of experiencing who we are in truth.

Karstein Bjastad

Stavanger, Norway

January, 2013

Acknowledgements

Firstly, I would like to thank my wife Lucy Johnson for her untiring support and dedication to help me bring this book to fruition. This book would probably not have seen the light of day without her support.

I would also like to thank Gary Renard for the workshop during which I had the insights that became the initial inspiration for this book, as well as his encouragement in the early days of the book's drafting process.

Chris Howe is another who helped me through the challenging early manuscript drafting process. And a special thank you to Fran Duda for guiding me into a space where the further writing process became a lot easier.

I would also like to thank Erik Laube, Elizabeth Griffin, Nouk Sanchez, Jelke Terpstra, D. Patrick Miller, Maria Barry, John Hunt and Maria Maloney for their assistance during the writing of this book.

Introduction

As a student of *A Course in Miracles*[1], one day I had a powerful realization about its teaching. The powerful realization was presented to me in the form of a mental picture.

As a reader of this book you may (i) currently be relatively new to spirituality; (ii) feel that your existing spiritual path takes you around in circles, or feels like a dead end; (iii) simply feel that there must be something more to spirituality than the teachings you have been exposed to seem to imply; and/or (iv) already be somewhat familiar with *A Course in Miracles* or another non-dualistic spiritual teaching, but feel the need to gain some new insights.

The aim of this book is in part to clarify and demystify what non-dualistic spirituality is, as well as give you practical tools to achieve what a non-dualistic spiritual teaching points toward. There are a number of misperceptions out there; misperceptions that lead to inconsistencies and confusion.

If you are unsure what a non-dualistic spiritual teaching is, don't worry. It will be made clear to you as you progress through this book. For now, let me just say that a non-dualistic spiritual teaching turns perceptions of reality upside down in a number of ways. As such, it often feels very counter intuitive in the early days of your exposure to it. So be warned, and mentally prepared, as we embark on demystifying non-dualistic spirituality.

There is a tendency to try to superimpose the message of a non-dualistic spiritual teaching onto our existing belief system. I have been guilty of this on numerous occasions. When I have what seem to me unanswered questions I often find this to be the reason. It is more a case of being unable to superimpose the non-dualistic spiritual teaching onto my pre-existing belief system. And remember, a non-dualistic spiritual teaching turns our perception of reality upside down in a number of ways. So the more you can put your existing belief system aside and focus purely on the message presented the easier it will be for you to appreciate the message.

This can seem like a bit too much of a leap of faith at first. But remember, you can always question it later when you have been given a more complete picture of the message. Being too quick to question it may prevent you from potentially finding the answer to one of your questions, which may be just around the corner as the teaching is further elaborated on.

I will use a number of analogies and metaphors to aid me in getting the relevant points across to you. Furthermore, I will devote a fair amount of space on how all the moving parts within the overall message hang together and how they fit into the bigger picture.

My introduction into the world of non-dualistic spirituality came via a self-study course called *A Course in Miracles* (or "ACIM" for short). It being a self-study course does not mean that you cannot study it with others. But it does mean that it is not set up with an organized teaching structure in a way that for example a religion is.

A Course in Miracles consists of a text section, a workbook section, a manual for teachers section and a clarification of terms section. While combined these sections are very comprehensive, ACIM is not written in a form that is easy for most people to get on with at first. Nor is the content described in a way that makes most people able to grasp its overall message easily. One of the aims of this book is to give you a flying start as you embark on a non-dualistic spiritual teaching. Or, if you are already familiar with one, to help you deepen your understanding of it. Having a clear understanding of how the different elements of an overall teaching hang together can in itself lead to questions you may have being answered.

As I stated at the start of this Introduction, I had a powerful realization about this teaching. This realization came in the form of a mental picture, and gave me a clearer appreciation of the nature of what is real and what is illusion, and their interrelationship. This clearer appreciation was a relief. It meant I could move forward with a greater degree of certainty and purpose.

Over time, as my appreciation for the deeper meaning of the mental picture that presented itself to me in my mind gained depth, seven Keys emerged. These seven Keys assist with the unraveling of the illusion. As such, they allow for the unfolding of an ever-deeper understanding of the *A Course in Miracles* teaching as well as non-dualistic spiritual teachings in general. Interestingly, but not surprisingly, once you gain a deeper understanding of one non-dualistic spiritual teaching, like ACIM, you find yourself able to grasp other non-dualistic spiritual teachings with relative ease. They all point to the same overarching truth.

In this book, I will share my powerful mental picture as well as the seven Keys with you. Each of the seven Keys will have a chapter dedicated to it. Furthermore, to aid with the application of a non-dualistic spiritual teaching, this book also focuses on giving you tools to implement in your daily life. This will include a practical exercise at the end of each chapter explaining a Key; allowing you to prepare your mind for later full application of the teaching provided, beyond what simply reading the text of the book would allow.

While it is important to understand a non-dualistic spiritual teaching intellectually in order to apply its teaching, an intellectual understanding with no related application of this understanding is of limited value. Implementing what you learn is essential in order to gain full benefit from the teaching. Hence, I encourage you to make good use of the exercises provided.

Chapter I

Reality and Illusion

Before we get into the seven Keys, let me present the mental picture that I find very powerful. This mental picture has helped me to gain an understanding of the conceptual framework within which the seven Keys work; it helped me to become aware of the hooks on which I can hang the seven Keys.

A non-dualistic spiritual teaching points to oneness; to the one Reality. And what is not within the one Reality is an Illusion. So what is Reality and what is Illusion?

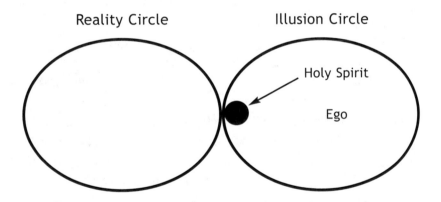

Reality Circle   Illusion Circle

Holy Spirit

Ego

In Reality, here shown as being inside the Reality Circle, everything is:

- Permanent;
- Unchanging;
- Eternal;
- Spirit (i.e. no form);
- Whole;
- Love (Unconditional);
- Peace;

- One;
- Knowing; and
- Creation.

The Illusion, or what is inside the Illusion Circle, includes:

- Form;
- Separation:
- Duality, as in good vs. bad, love (conditional) vs. hate, up vs. down, right vs. wrong, etc.;
- Time;
- Space;
- Judgment;
- Perception;
- Lack; and
- Energy.

The Illusion, or Illusion Circle, has one more element, represented by the small black ball on the inside of the Illusion Circle, where it touches the Reality Circle. You can look at this small black ball as an eye's pupil looking into the Reality Circle. We will refer to this small black ball, or "pupil", as the Holy Spirit. As such, the Holy Spirit is able to "see" into the Reality Circle. This book will also at times refer to the Holy Spirit as remembering the Reality Circle, or remembering Reality.

We call the non-Holy Spirit part of the Illusion Circle the ego. Be clear on this definition of the ego, as it differs from the definition of the ego in e.g. psychology.

When I first connected with this realization as a mental picture, I found it a simple yet very practical guiding symbol. Together with the seven Keys, it helps me to regain my awareness of (i) who I am in truth; (ii) why I am here; and (iii) how I can regain my experience of who I am in truth. We will touch on all those three points later in the book.

To me, simplicity is a good sign. Complexity often hides unhelpful noise that somehow deliberately finds its way into the equation, with the sole purpose of creating confusion. The ego is the part of the Illusion that wants complexity and confusion. The ego wants you to think of the Illusion as reality, and it wants to maintain a certain complexity and a certain level of confusion within the Illusion's make-up in order to help it achieve this.

The Reality Circle is who you are in truth and where you are in truth. The Reality Circle is your true self. The Illusion Circle is where the ego has made you think you are.

The two circles are mutually exclusive; they are not overlapping[1]. There is no room for Reality in the Illusion Circle. Nor is there room for Illusion in the Reality Circle. Luckily though, within the Illusion Circle we have the Holy Spirit. You will discover that the Holy Spirit is a vital tool in the uncovering of your true self. More about this later.

The pictorial representation of the Illusion and Reality Circles has proved useful to me for picturing in my mind the mutually exclusive nature of Reality and Illusion, as well as visually getting a sense of how the Holy Spirit fits into the overall picture.

As has now been described, we are in truth in Reality. Whilst there, we are kind of dreaming about being in the Illusion. Hence, the much used term in spirituality of awakening; our aim is to awaken from the dream about being in the Illusion, so we can see that it is no more real than our nocturnal dreams. Nocturnal dreams may feel real while we are in the middle of experiencing them. But as soon as we wake up, we realize they are not. This is also true for our dream about being in the Illusion. Once we awaken, and experience our true self, we will come to realize that the Illusion dream was not real either. So, metaphorically speaking, we can say that our aim is to awaken from the dream of being in the Illusion Circle.

In this book, I will primarily use the terms Reality and Illusion, rather than Reality Circle and Illusion Circle, respectively, since these terms are closer to the terminology used in *A Course in Miracles*, and some of you may already be familiar with *A Course in Miracles*, or may read it at some point. With this in mind, let me also reconcile the ACIM definitions with the terminology used in this book.

Reality, or the Reality Circle, is what *A Course in Miracles* refers to as reality, and also as God, Source, Heaven and the Kingdom.

Illusion, or the Illusion Circle, is referred to in *A Course in Miracles* as illusion. ACIM splits the illusion into two main parts; (i) the Holy Spirit, which is also referred to as Jesus in places; and (ii) the ego, in the same way as this book splits the Illusion, or Illusion Circle, into the Holy Spirit and the ego.

This book uses the ego term in the same way as *A Course in Miracles* uses it, the part of your mind that wants to control you. The ego also wants to keep your level of emotional pain under control, but with no means, nor any intentions, of getting rid of your emotional pain[2]. Instead, all the while it stays focused on preventing you from experiencing yourself in Reality, or God, Source, Heaven or the Kingdom. More on this as we get into the Keys.

This book also uses the Holy Spirit term in the same way as ACIM uses the Holy Spirit and Jesus. Within the ACIM there are references to the Holy Spirit as both a memory of God[3] and as being able to see God[4].

Thus far you have been presented with the mental picture of the Reality Circle and the Illusion Circle. This gives you the larger conceptual framework within which the essence of a non-dualistic spiritual teaching resides. At the more detailed everyday experiential level, the seven Keys will help you along this journey like guiding beacons, putting the spotlight on the ego thought system, and thereby help you to look through it and past it. So let's next look at how we can get to experience who we are in truth with the help of the seven Keys, the first of which is: "it is all in the mind".

Let me clarify here, just to make sure this is clear, that there are concepts other than the ones I will present in this book that can successfully guide you to experience your true self. And there are teachings other than *A Course in Miracles* that can achieve this. However, since you have come across this book and have started to read it, odds are that there is something within this mental picture and these seven Keys that will speak to you in a way that resonates at a deeper level; and as such will help guide you towards unraveling the ego, and with it the whole Illusion. When fully unraveled, your true self will be uncovered and you can experience your naked truth as it is.

Chapter 2

It is All in the Mind

Let's get into the first Key: **It is all in the mind**. But what does this actually mean? And what are the ramifications of everything being in the mind?

Well, for starters it means that anything you see out there with your seeming eyes is not actually out there. Rather, it is in your mind. Talk of our perceptions being back to front, since this is certainly not our conscious experience. Rather, our daily experiences would seem to contradict this. Our experience is more one of what is out there, the world, filling our mind, and not of the world being filled *by* our mind.

Some of you may have heard it stated in other spiritual teachings too that it is all in your mind. These teachings may or may not have gone on to state what this actually means as far as your thought processes are concerned. Either way, we will look at that in this book.

In order to gain a good grounding from which to understand that *it is all in the mind*, let's look at how the ego came to be. You are in Reality, feeling whole and totally cared for. The concept of a concern in any shape or form does not exist. But somehow you seemed to become attracted to this idea of autonomy; of having your own separate identity as opposed to being all that is together with all the rest of all that is. This autonomy concept seemed to create an experience of exactly this; a conscious experience of being your own identity away from the whole and the complete. Your conscious experience became one of being separate from Reality. This experience of separation from Reality made you feel guilty. You felt guilty because you were completely loved and cared for in Reality, and yet you did not seem to sufficiently appreciate what you had. Now you experience yourself as being outside of this; all alone and very exposed.

Since by your very nature you are creative, this seeming autonomy thought, however innocently intended, seemed to take on a mind of its own. In effect, it seemed to create a mind of its own; a separate mind. However, creation is only possible in Reality, within the Reality Circle. And creation can only extend itself. Creation is also permanent and unchanging in nature. What is happening here with the Illusion is that something completely new is arising. Not only is it new, but it is also able to change. Both of which, new and changing, are impossible in Reality. So this seemingly created mind is not actually created at all. It is a make believe construct. Therefore, rather than referring to it as being created, let us say that it has been made. The distinction between being made and being created is one that is also made in *A Course in Miracles*[1]. It is important to be clear on the distinction between created and made[2]. Within the Illusion, which is where this seeming new mind is being made, everything that appears to manifest is made, as opposed to created. And what is made is forever changing and has a finite life; change and death is a certainty.

This made up mind is split into two component parts. One part sees, or remembers, Reality and the other part does not remember the true nature of Reality. We refer to the part that has forgotten the nature of Reality as the ego and the part that remembers Reality as the Holy Spirit. The ego snowballs by weaving more and more made up thoughts to its construct. It puts in place an ever larger web of misperceptions. Thus, the split mind becomes correspondingly more biased away from the Holy Spirit; away from the part of itself that remembers Reality.

However, since in truth you are in Reality; in the Reality Circle, and Reality is eternally unchanging, under no circumstances can you lose your awareness of what Reality is. Within the Illusion dream, the only thing that changes in this regard is your level of conscious awareness, or remembrance, of the truth of Reality.

So your daily experiences, the Illusion, is a dream, a sleight of hand. To use a much used cinema analogy; what you experience as being out there in the world is something you are projecting onto your screen; where the world is the screen and your mind is the projector. The part of your mind engaging in this projection is the ego.

Looking at it from the perspective of being in the movie theater, when you watch something on the movie screen that upsets you, and you would like to change it, you do not go up to the screen and try to change things there. This is because you know that the images on the screen are projected from a projector at the back of the movie theater. Instead, if you could, you would go to the projector and change what is in it. The same is the case for your life in the world. We keep trying to arrange objects and people out there in the world. We do this since, contrary to knowing that what we see on the screen in the movie theater is a projection from a projector, we still think that objects, including bodies, out there in the world are real. We have forgotten that they are projected from the mind. If we want to change those projected images we need to go to where they are projected from; our mind. We need to make changes in our mind. We need to change our mind about the world[3]. While we cannot go and change the content in the projector while in the movie theater, the good news is that we can change our mind about what we project from our mind, and hence what appears on the screen of the world. On the topic of changing your mind, please be informed that the word repent in the Bible comes from *metanoia* in the Greek version of the Bible, which means 'change of mind'.

As we progress through the seven Keys, practical tools are provided to correct the misperceptions you have allowed into your mind, and continue to allow into your mind. All these misperceptions are there in order to satisfy the ego part of your mind, to keep that part of your mind satisfied that it is in control.

The ego likes to be in control of your life. In its pursuit for control, it has gotten to the point where the ego is now your perceived identity. And the ego has convinced you that the last thing you want to do is to lose this identity, or rather what you have been duped into believing is your identity. It becomes afraid if it feels it is losing control over you. A number of spiritual teachings do not ruffle the ego's feathers much. The ego knows that those teachings will allow it to retain its control. However, the Keys get under the ego's skin. They make the ego scared[4]. In order to stop you in your tracks, the ego will ask many questions, hoping that at least some of them will remain unanswered and make you confused enough to discontinue your interest in this teaching. If the ego's questions will not achieve this objective, it will try other tactics. This is because if you truly apply the Keys the ego will lose control over you, and it can sense this. Therefore, I encourage you to watch your thoughts very closely for the antics of the ego. As we get further into the book, you will gain a better sense of how to watch out for these antics.

Let's talk a bit about how the Holy Spirit operates within the Illusion, within the world. A picture that works well for me is a pyramid or a cone. You can think of the Holy Spirit as the epicenter. Around it, at the bottom, you have individual beings. All these beings have a connection, like an invisible string, connecting them to the Holy Spirit, represented by the epicenter of the pyramid or cone. Through these invisible strings of connections up to the epicenter of the pyramid or cone we are all connected to the Holy Spirit. And through the Holy Spirit, we are all connected to each other. While we all connect to the same memory of Reality, we will at different times and as seemingly different individual beings, connect to different contents of the memory of Reality, which memory the Holy Spirit represents. Since *it is all in the mind,* while we seem to connect as bodies, it is through the mind our connection actually takes place.

I would like to take this concept one step further. There is a tendency to want to think of the Holy Spirit as something above us, something higher up in the hierarchy than us. But remember, the Holy Spirit is a part of us. To think of it in hierarchical terms can give us the implicit sense that it is not part of us; that it is outside of us. Therefore, I like to think of the pyramid or cone as being collapsed into a flat circle, bringing the Holy Spirit down to the ground level, with the Holy Spirit at the circle's center and all individuals at its periphery. This also shows the powerful connection we can have with people when we connect with them through the Holy Spirit, our common denominator within the Illusion; a common denominator that remembers Reality, remembers who we are in truth. The Holy Spirit remembers the oneness we all are in truth. Connecting with people, or other sentient beings, through the Holy Spirit and thereby involving our memory of Reality while interacting with another is an example of what *A Course in Miracles* refers to as a Holy Instant.

Collapsing the pyramid, or cone, into a flat circle also helps us to get a sense of the equality of all things. Understanding and appreciating that everything is equal is fundamental for understanding a non-dualistic spiritual teaching. It is also fundamental for being at peace[5]. The alternative to non-equality leads to competition, a breeding ground for conflict[6].

So the Holy Spirit sees/remembers Reality and can remind us of it. However, the Illusion cannot be reconciled with the truth of Reality. The two are mutually exclusive, as represented by the Reality Circle/Illusion Circle illustration in Chapter 1. Therefore, while our conscious awareness is of the Illusion we are unable to have an *experience* that exactly matches Reality. However, the Holy Spirit; the *memory* of Reality, resides in the Illusion and is familiar with our experience of being in the Illusion. Since there is no time in Reality, the Holy Spirit also remembers eternity, i.e. no time. As such, the Holy Spirit is able to operate within the Illusion outside of the constraints of linear time. As far as all seeming individual lives are concerned, the Holy Spirit knows what has gone before and what lies ahead. And it knows our goal, to know ourselves in truth. Therefore, the Holy Spirit has all the ingredients necessary to lead us along the path we want to walk. It will do so by communicating with us at the level we are at in our spiritual understanding and development.

I would like to mention that since *A Course in Miracles* teaches the thought system of the Holy Spirit it is about oneness and oneness only. However, you will find a lot of dualistic language in ACIM. Why? Because this is how we think. This is what we can relate to in light our daily experience and spiritual development. We think in dualistic terms. Things are good or bad, we love and hate, etc. In other words, our predominant way of thinking has an element of judgment, and comparing and contrasting. How else can you make up your mind as to whether something is good or bad, healthy or unhealthy, useful or not, etc., etc.? The message of *A Course in Miracles* meets us where our thinking is. Equally, the Holy Spirit meets us where our thinking is. This is where we are receptive to messages from which we can learn and be directed towards a non-dualistic understanding; and ultimately a non-dualistic experience. As such, dualistic statements used are metaphors. In pure non-dualism there is nothing to judge. Everything just is, and all is known to all of itself as the oneness that it is. It is important to be aware of this since two sentences like "Your fellow human beings are here to act as a mirror for you to learn about yourself" would seem to contradict a statement like "You are the only one here". But they do not contradict each other since the former is a dualistic statement of comparing and contrasting as a means to point you towards oneness, while the latter is a non-dualistic statement of oneness. To say they contradict each other would be like comparing apples and oranges.

I would also like to point out that the Holy Spirit is your Higher Self, or Highest Self. And yes, this means that there is only one Higher Self; one Higher Self to which we as seemingly different individuals connect with different parts of. The parts we connect with as seeming individuals depend on our own *unique path*, a path that is a function of our unique web of misperceptions. More on this later. However, we all move towards a *common goal*, a goal that is also the Holy Spirit's goal; the goal of knowing and experiencing ourselves in truth; the one truth of the Reality that we all are.

Hence, contrary to the impression you may be left with by other spiritual teachings, you do not have your own individual higher self. Your Higher Self is the epicenter of the pyramid or the cone, or the center of the collapsed pyramid or cone, to which all individual beings are connected. The ego would love for you to think that you have your own individual higher self. That would give it the perfect hook to let you dabble in your spirituality while at the same time safely remain within its grasp; a grasp based on separation and a sense of individuality. Any spiritual aspirations that maintain the sense of separation are perfect fodder for the ego. And if your *highest* aspirations are left to the guidance of something that itself is considered unique to you then that would be the ego's perfect spiritual combo!

There is one more thing I would like to mention in connection with the Holy Spirit at times being referred to as a memory. Some people think of the memory as being passive only. While here, we refer to the memory of Reality as something active. If you already think of your memory as active, you can skip to the next paragraph. For those of you who think of your memory as passive, think about what happens in your mind when you are faced with a question. Granted, typically you search your mind, or your memory, for an answer. However, there are also times when an answer is presented to you in your mind. The answer just pops into your mind. This is an example of your memory also being able to play an active role when you are looking for an answer.

Getting back to the concept of a split mind, in the Illusion defined as being split between the Holy Spirit and the ego, let us also remind ourselves that at some level even the ego part of the split mind knows that there is only one of itself. That is why you often feel bad if you do something untoward to another. A conscious part of your mind often feels negativity around this because a deeper, and unconscious, part of your mind experiences it as an attack on itself. The corollary is of course also true. If you do something that is uplifting to another you tend to feel uplifted yourself. By the way, no action is required for this to be the overall effect and for you to potentially sense this at a conscious level. Remember, *it is all in the mind*. Thoughts have power in their own right. As we are reminded in Gary Renard's book *The Disappearance of the Universe*: "What you do isn't the important thing, even though it is a *result* of what you think. It's what you think that will either keep you dreaming or help you get home, not what you do."[7] Ultimately *it is all in the mind*. Thoughts are of the mind. Action is just the execution or expression of a thought. So action or no action following a thought, the thought itself has an effect on the mind, on the one mind. In light of this you may want to become a bit more careful about how you think about others!

Related to this topic is the topic of many people feeling burnt out by their efforts to help others. You are here to be truly helpful[8], but our everyday perspective of what is helpful does not always correspond to being *truly* helpful. Remember, there is only one Holy Spirit, only one Higher Self. The Holy Spirit is here to guide us all home in the way most helpful to each seeming individual, which depends on their respective ego mind's web of misperceptions. While you can wish for the higher good of all who cross your path, you should take care to connect with your intuition or gut feel about what actions to take in relation to people. They have certain life experiences for certain reasons. Sometimes you can assist people along their path by taking certain actions, and sometimes they are better assisted along their path by you not taking action. The experiences the Holy Spirit has in mind for them are on occasion helped by you taking action and on occasion hindered. Having thoughts and taking actions that are aligned with the Holy Spirit, are aligned with love for yourself and this other person, will keep you energized. While the opposite is prone to burn you out. I have chosen to bring this to your attention here. However, I would also ask you not to dwell much on it at this stage. As you work through these Keys and gain a better understanding of your path ahead, your loving intuition and gut feeling will improve. I will re-introduce the topic of being truly helpful in the chapter about the sixth Key.

A Course in Miracles is a course about the mind[9]. A lot of people try to use the principles of *A Course in Miracles* on the level of form. The level of form is not something ACIM concerns itself with per se. So do not fall into the trap of using a non-dualistic spiritual teaching to manifest your next car, your perfect partner or the next house. The ego would love for you to fall into this trap. But do not give it that satisfaction, which leads nicely to the second Key: "there is no form, only content".

Exercise

Before we go to the second Key, let's look at a practical way in which you can start your mind training using the first Key; *it is all in the mind*. *It is all in the mind* means that your body is in your mind; even your brain is in your mind. The mind is the cause, and everything else is the effect. Thus, change your mind about something (cause) and you change your perception of that something (effect). Start practicing and experimenting with this Key today. Become mindful of experiences in your daily life, and acknowledge that they are projections from your mind. As you do this, make a mental or written note of your thoughts about the workings of the ego projections from your mind.

Chapter 3

There is No Form, Only Content

So, the second Key is: **There is no form, only content.**

In Reality there is no form. When the ego first had a seeming experience of itself there was also no form. The seeming experience of form arose later.

The Evolution of the Ego

The ego induced feeling of being outside of the Reality Circle and all alone[1] and rejected[2] was scary in itself. This soon became intensified by another scary thought, the thought that Reality, which by now the ego has objectified into a separate entity that we generally refer to as God, is angry with the ego for leaving it; for the ego's lack for appreciation of what was provided for it there. And that Reality, or God, will probably avenge itself if the ego were caught not repenting or if it were to return to Reality. These thoughts became increasingly painful; to the point where they were too painful to endure. So the ego decided that the Illusion Circle needed to hide, and hide well. Eventually, a remedying thought came into the ego part of the split Illusion mind; a remedy that would allow the ego to hide from Reality in such a way that the chance of being found by Reality, or God, was extremely remote. It would also allow the acute mental pain of the guilt and fear, that the ego is by now experiencing, to be off-loaded; in a way diluted. The solution that came into the ego part of the mind was to make matter, or form, and to scatter itself into a near infinite number of parts. This would allow for the mental pain to be distributed across a number of mini-minds, or mind fragments. It would allow an individual mini-mind that feels emotional pain in connection with the initial guilt and fear, or for any other seeming reason for that matter, to offload this emotional pain by projecting it onto another part of the mind within this seeming manifestation. The implementation of this remedying thought set off what is generally known as the Big Bang, and made the universe of multiplicity, time and space[3].

The ego part of your mind does not remember Reality. The ego remembers that there is Reality, of which it is very afraid and feels guilty for leaving, but it has forgotten everything *about* Reality. Because of its guilt and fear about what the ego thinks Reality is, the ego is guarding its intricate thought system like a hawk. This intricate thought system with the ability to project is also what provides the ego with a bearable experience; a numbing down of, and a decoy from, its intrinsic emotional pain.

One thing that is important to appreciate is that while the ego mind has made what appears as multiplicity, the mind is in fact still the *one* seeming split mind; split between (i) the Holy Spirit part that remembers Reality; and (ii) the ego part that has forgotten the true nature of Reality, and tries to hide from it. Anything the ego does is a sleight of hand; an illusionary construct. The ego provides an optical illusion of form and multiplicity. The original seeming thought of autonomy, referenced in the previous chapter, generated a seeming experience of such autonomy away from Reality. However, despite any further attempts to make it appear differently, the ego mind is still one, and, as mentioned in the previous chapter, at some level the ego experiences itself and knows itself as one. This means that in its attempt to lessen its sense of emotional pain through multiplicity, the ego mind is in effect just recycling it around the place whenever it is projecting, since through the act of projection the mind as a whole never actually gets rid of any emotional pain. The tools we will get into later are alternatives to projection and will make emotional pain leave the mind altogether. After all, emotional pain is trash not worthy of recycling.

A Course in Miracles advises us that no thought is neutral[4]. The majority of our thoughts are fueled by some sort of emotion, an emotion rooted in the original emotions of guilt and fear that occurred at the inception of the split mind. Such thoughts form our perceived individuality. And they tend to seek the experience of specialness and uniqueness. Individuality breeds individuality. Once we have bought into all this individuality stuff we feel we need to maintain it. Oh, is the ego happy about this! This often leads to some sort of battle with others because resources are experienced as limited. There are certain boys/girls you are interested in, there is only so much money going around, jobs are in short supply, etc. So you get me versus you and me up against you. You get us versus them, my country versus your country. The list goes on. And it is all a form of denial, a denial ultimately rooted in the denial of who you are in truth. Denying that we are all the same, and denying the guilt and fear associated with making the Illusion. This denial is seeking an expression; which by its very nature denial has to do. The way it expresses itself in the world is through the mechanism of projection.

Your Ego Experience

Fast-forwarding to today, all emotions in life that upset your peace of mind are ultimately rooted in the original guilt and fear. And every ego thought you have is symbolic of the original seeming experience of separation from Reality.

In your mind you have denied the original guilt and fear, and guilt and fear have become your strongest emotions. It is a well-known concept in psychology that what you have denied will show up as some sort of projection. Once something is denied, it will eventually show up as a projection onto someone or something else. This denial gives temporary relief from emotional pain. If you have done something wrong and you are confronted with your wrongdoing, this is likely to give rise to emotional pain. However, if you are able to convince yourself and this person confronting you that it was someone else's fault that you made this mistake, then you will feel less emotional pain. This need to find a scapegoat is sometimes conscious. But oftentimes it is unconscious. It is just something you typically do in these situations, as though you are on autopilot. There is something within you that will not allow you to admit certain mistakes. These patterns of behavior are rooted in denials; denials that typically are below the surface of what you are consciously aware of. They are typically in your sub-conscious mind. The original guilt and fear is at the root of all the denied emotions that cause you emotional pain.

Furthermore, what you project onto the screen of the world is what will shape your perceptions[5]. The perception of everything you see or otherwise sense in the world, including the above mentioned perceived individuality and perceptions of limited availability of potential partners, money, jobs, etc. comes from projections caused by denials in your mind, most of which are in your sub-conscious mind. Hence, your perceptions ultimately come from your denials too.

But at the end of the day there is no one else out there. At the end of the day, we need nothing as we have everything in Reality. We may have an experience of there being a multitude of separate individuals with their own individual needs. We may perceive there to be a lot of stuff in our lives and a multitude of things going on. And it may give us temporary relief from emotional pain to project onto another. But a perception is all it is. It seems like reality but it is not. All it is, is the made up Illusion regurgitating itself; doing its merry-go-round.

To the ego, this makes the whole setup foolproof. However, the memory we have of Reality, the Holy Spirit, is more than capable of guiding us out of this insanity.

Undoing the Ego

On your path towards your goal of knowing yourself in truth you will eliminate emotional pain. As we are reminded in Gary

Renard's *The Disappearance of the Universe*; "That is why [ACIM] wants to help people realize what's in their unconscious – so they can rid of it. Most people, especially nice, spiritual people, don't know about the murderous thought system that runs this universe, or the hatred that's underneath the surface of their mind. Nor do most of them want to know. Most people just want everything to be honky-dory. You can't blame them for wanting peace, but *real* peace is found by undoing the ego, not by covering it over."[6]

So the ego, and with it your unconscious mind, is what you seem to be up against. Although a figment of your imagination, it nonetheless seems very real. Even quantum physics has come to the conclusion that the universe cannot possibly exist, other than as a concept of the mind.

You will not be able to unravel the ego within the Illusion unless you look its thought system squarely in the eye *together with* the Holy Spirit, together with the part of your Illusion experience that knows of the ego's non-existence, and remembers Reality. In looking at your thoughts with the Holy Spirit you are an observer, observing the thoughts of the ego. Since we are so closely identified with the ego we are in effect, together with the Holy Spirit, training ourselves to *observe* who we think we are; who our day-to-day experience tells us that we are. Remember, non-dualistic spirituality is mind training.

The Keys will help you undo the ego. It will be achieved through utilizing your understanding of the nothingness of the Illusion and the ego; and, with the help of the Holy Spirit, starting to observe it as such. As will be revealed through the seven Keys, with the help of the Holy Spirit you will wake up from the dream by lovingly divesting your attachment from the story fed you by the ego; lovingly divesting yourself from your belief in the Illusion. Together with the Holy Spirit you will keep chipping away at the ego and its presented version of life, until the ego features no more in your mind.

Let's now take our focus to Reality and remind ourselves that the content of Reality is love, unconditional love, unending love. Everything in Reality is eternal and whole. In addition, Reality is holographic. Holographic means that all parts of the whole contain the whole. In the case of Reality, this means that love contains peace, happiness, creation, etc. Equally, happiness contains love, peace, creation, etc. In truth, Reality just is. And the content of Reality just is. It has no form, it just is. The assignment of individual attributes is just a teaching tool. And any time one attribute of Reality is mentioned in effect all its attributes are implicitly mentioned.

The Holy Spirit is your memory of your content, of your true essence.

In spiritual teachings in general, you may come across terms like spirit, the divine, inner wisdom and guidance, universal intelligence, among others. These are all pointing towards the formless, while also pointing towards the content of love.

When something in *A Course in Miracles* is mentioned as having form, such a statement is a metaphor. Our conscious experience is one of living in the world. Unless the path to our goal, our goal being experiencing ourselves in truth, is described in terms consistent with our conscious experience of the world, such descriptions will have limited if any teaching value. Therefore, since we have made a setup consisting largely of form within the Illusion, the Holy Spirit makes use of this framework to make teaching tools. These teaching tools enable us to move towards our experience of Reality. And Reality is who, what and where we are in truth.

This brings to mind something that can be confusing at first. You may have heard, or you may hear in the future, an *A Course in Miracles'* teacher stating that the Holy Spirit is not concerned with actions in the world. You may also hear the same teacher or another teacher of *A Course in Miracles* stating that the Holy Spirit inspires you to take action in the world. These are both true statements.

I can feel your confusion arising while writing this. Let me tell you why they are both true. The Holy Spirit is not concerned with actions taken in the world per se, nor what happens in the world. But it is its function to guide you along the path to awakening to your experience of who you are in truth. In order to achieve this you have to learn certain lessons. The Holy Spirit will inspire you and others to take actions that will result in events unfolding that give you and others an opportunity to learn these lessons. Therefore, the Holy Spirit is not concerned with actions in the world per se. It is there to act as your guide in the world. As such, the Holy Spirit will inspire you to take actions that will lead to learning opportunities. It is not the action that is the driving force for this but rather the potential for learning a lesson.

The Holy Spirit will give you as many opportunities as it takes to learn a certain lesson[7]. In the ego script each opportunity to learn the lesson will be accompanied by a 'convenient' excuse as to why you do not want, or feel ready, to learn this lesson now. But the Holy Spirit will remind you each time that if a lesson is presented to you it is *because* you are ready to learn it. It will further remind you that what has given rise to the need to learn this lesson is your seeming adventure into form, while in truth you are in Reality; in essence you are eternal unconditional love. Furthermore, the lesson has ultimately arisen out of your unconscious guilt and fear, neither of which is real. The manifestation of the lesson is therefore only symbolic of what is in your unconscious mind, rather than an example of who you are in truth. You are now ready to learn the presented lesson by mentally releasing to the Holy Spirit what brought about the lesson, whether this was brought about by something you saw or something someone said or did.

With this mindset and understanding, you can choose to learn a lesson when it is first presented to you. You can choose to mentally release the related thought pattern and/or event to the Holy Spirit. And through this mental release a part of your unconscious mind, ultimately rooted in your unconscious guilt and fear, is released. I will elaborate further on how this mental process and the related release are achieved later in the book, once you have been presented with all the seven Keys. But for now let me add that the Holy Spirit will always point you away from identification with and attachment to form and towards content, the content of Reality; content that is pure unconditional love, your true content.

The Holy Spirit is all about giving. Content can be given freely without loss. In fact, you gain by giving; giving becomes receiving. This is why you often hear about the Holy Spirit operating through extension or expansion. At the level of content this is what happens when you give. If you truly give love, joy, happiness, etc., it gives a heightened sense of the same in you. On the level of form this is of course different. If you take money out of your pocket and give it to someone you will have less money in your pocket afterwards. If you give someone your only watch, you will be left with no watch. However, the level of form can be used by the Holy Spirit to give you an experience of expansion in a way that you can more easily and readily relate to. You may make someone happy by giving them money. This may make you happy too. In addition the Holy Spirit, through the construct of the physical universe, may arrange for some money to come your way in excess of what you gave away. There may be an unexpected positive development in your business that is financially lucrative to you. So be open-minded about how your lessons may transpire for you, even in the context of giving and receiving on the level of form. All the while remember that non-dualistic spirituality is mind training, and that giving and receiving is the same at the level of the mind. There is only one mind, so how could it be any different?

Our experience though is one of form, and an experience of

living in the world. So it is useful to ask the question of what the world is for. The answer depends on what part of your mind you ask. If you ask the ego part of your mind, it will tell you that the world is here to show you that the separation is real. If you ask the Holy Spirit, it will tell you that the world is here to show you the innocence of all beings and things.

The ego will have you believe that you have separated from Reality, and that the feeling of guilt and fear in connection with this separation is real. The Holy Spirit will tell you that you never separated from Reality, that you in truth are still there, and that everything in the seeming world can be seen as testament to your guiltlessness, or innocence, if only you take the time to look it all squarely in the eye together with the Holy Spirit.

Once all your lessons in the world have been learned you will see only innocence in the world, and you will some time thereafter lay aside your form, your body, for the last time. Form is only here as a teaching tool. Once all lessons are learned and your experience is one of innocence and unconditional love only, and your mind is completely at peace, there is no longer a need for teaching tools. At this point the purpose of form has gone. With it all trace of form will eventually leave your mind[8]. Your mind will then only experience content, the content of who you are in truth, Reality itself only. I say 'only', but it is in fact 'all'. Remember, Reality is all there is and the Illusion isn't[9].

The portrayal of a person, including its soul, as completely leaving the Illusion upon learning all its lessons raised questions in my mind in the earlier days of my exposure to ACIM. *A Course in Miracles* implies that Jesus learned all his lessons and is the person behind the words in ACIM. And a number of ACIM teachers will state that this is so. This seems at odds with the notion that Jesus is no longer in the Illusion. The Holy Spirit is in the Illusion. But Jesus, having supposedly achieved the goal of leaving the Illusion behind, and as such laid his body aside for the last time, can no longer be in the Illusion, period. This preoccupied my mind for some time. It often held me back from studying the ACIM material. So for a while the ego had me just where it wanted me; somewhat paralyzed by my ego inspired questioning. However, I have since come to realize that both perspectives are for all intents and purposes correct. I do not wish the ego the pleasure of potentially paralyzing you with this question, so let me share with you why we have these seemingly diametrically opposed statements. What I often find with the Holy Spirit is that I can get one part of an answer early on. And later, when I am ready and receptive to it, I will receive a more complete picture.

Before I present the answer, please be reminded that the aim of the Holy Spirit is to get us out of this seeming Illusion. In addition, we have to remember that everything in the Illusion is a projection. It is not actually there. Any given physical projection can be of either the Holy Spirit or the ego.

The Holy Spirit will do what is most effective to get us to learn our lessons. Actually, I should be careful with using the term 'learning our lessons' since in fact there is nothing we need to learn. We are in truth completely whole and at home in Reality. So our lessons within the Illusion are lessons in unlearning, or peeling away, all that we have seemingly added to our mind during our imagined journey in the world[10]. For a lot of us, what has been added to our mind on our journey has been added, directly or indirectly, by religion; if not in this lifetime, then in an earlier one. And a lot of the information that has come into our mind from this source is keeping us stuck here. For a large number of readers of A Course in Miracles the religion they have been most exposed to is Christianity. This does not mean that the message in A Course in Miracles is not universal and is not applicable to all. It is universal and applicable to all. But what it does mean is that it contains a lot of Christian terminology. Each Christian term used is re-defined and Jesus' teaching is restated so that Jesus' message while he walked the earth can be properly understood. Jesus' contemporaries did not fully understand his teaching. The religion made in Jesus' name reflects this. Hence, as a teaching tool, the Holy Spirit presented itself, sometimes implicitly and sometimes explicitly, as Jesus as it brought forth the material of *A Course in Miracles*. The Jesus who walked the earth understood everything that is stated in *A Course in Miracles*. Jesus, for the last years of his earthly life, was completely at one with the Holy Spirit. He became a pure communication instrument for the Holy Spirit, and as such became synonymous with the Holy Spirit. Jesus' mind was like a deflated Illusion Circle where all that was left was the black dot symbolizing the Holy Spirit.

Once Jesus' body stopped working, Jesus left the Illusion behind and as such never again needed another body. He achieved the experience of only being in Reality, of being at one with Reality. So the world with all its teaching tools had become redundant to him. Jesus the soul, as we tend to think of individual expressions of beings beyond the body, is no more. Sightings of Jesus in the flesh after his seeming death are examples of the Holy Spirit making a physical projection. If you have read Gary Renard's book *The Disappearance of the Universe*, taking your mind back to this book will remind you of Arten and Pursah as other examples where the Holy Spirit made physical projections. But there is no Jesus as such out there to relay the teachings of the Jesus who walked the earth.

This might seem like a deception on the part of the Holy Spirit at first. But remember that Jesus the body and Jesus the soul were also just projections within the Illusion. They never actually were. Only Reality is.

The Holy Spirit remembers you and sees you and everything else as innocent and perfect[11]. The world out there is a projected world of symbols, symbols of what is predominantly contained in the ego part of the split mind. While the Holy Spirit sees the innocence and perfection in you it also knows that you are not consciously aware of it. The Holy Spirit uses the symbols in the world, past as well as present symbols, as tools to help you towards becoming aware of your own innocence and perfection[12]. And the concept of right versus wrong is not a part of the Holy Spirit's thinking. As stated already, the Holy Spirit just wants you to get it, get that you are already innocent and perfect. And whichever symbol is the more helpful in order for you to get this is the symbol the Holy Spirit will use, which remember is actually a memory of yours; a memory of who you are in truth. For providing the content of *A Course in Miracles*, the Holy Spirit deemed the symbol of Jesus to be the best symbol to use.

Some people are abstract minded. For them something abstract like the Holy Spirit, or just Spirit, might be the most helpful symbol. To others a more concrete symbol is more helpful, like Jesus, mother Mary, Buddha or another person symbolizing the same qualities as the Holy Spirit. Looking specifically at *A Course in Miracles* you find what seems like inconsistencies between how the symbols of Holy Spirit and Jesus are used. While ACIM generally states that Jesus and the Holy Spirit are the same the two are also referred to as being different[13]. But remember, all dualistic statements in *A Course in Miracles* are metaphors. And ACIM caters for a wide audience. Some are abstract minded, some are scientific minded and there are a whole host of mind inclinations in between. Therefore, a different use of metaphors on what is largely the same topic is used to get the message across to a broad spectrum of different minded people.

What is ultimately important is that the meaning to *you* of *your* chosen symbol of the Holy Spirit is consistent with its real function. The symbol's real function is to *remove* the blocks, or misperceptions, in your mind that obscures it from perceiving who you are in truth[14], and, as these blocks are removed, lead you to the *experience* of who you are in truth.

You may use more than one symbol to represent the Holy Spirit. While most people use the same symbol every time they connect with the Holy Spirit, you may find that one symbol is more powerful in one instance while in another instance another symbol is more powerful.

You want to choose the symbol that is the most powerful vehicle for you to communicate in a more conscious manner with the part of your mind that remembers who you are in truth, whether this is an abstract symbol, e.g. the Holy Spirit, or a concrete symbol, e.g. Jesus.

You may already have become comfortable with such a symbol or you may still be working towards it. Either way, all is good. This brings us to the third Key: "there are no coincidences".

Exercise

Again, before we move onto the next Key, let's look at a practical way in which you can start your mind training using the second Key; *there is no form, only content*. *There is no form, only content* tells us that form is not real; anything that appears to happen in the world of form is not actually happening. Only Reality, with its content, is real. In Reality is where you really are. So practice the following: every time you become upset or feel fear or anxiety, remind yourself of the non-reality of it; none of it is actually happening. You are safely in Reality. Hand whatever made you upset, fearful or anxious over to the Holy Spirit. Make a mental or written note of your experiences.

Chapter 4

There are No Coincidences

So, the third Key is: **There are no coincidences**. How great is that? Well, if there are no coincidences we can just relax. And a relaxed mind is more able to stay in the now and be open to communication from the Holy Spirit. So, just relax into it all!

The Holy Spirit knows our fastest way home. At the same time the ego knows that as soon as you find your home it will no longer have a home. This is what is behind the internal battle we all face in this world.

One of our aims is to develop a good communication channel with the Holy Spirit; to move towards less ego noise. We want to listen to the gentle, loving and reassuring voice of the Holy Spirit, our memory of home, our memory of who we are in truth.

When the time and circumstances are right, the Holy Spirit will set in motion a synchronistic sequence of thoughts and events, all of which have the potential to move you along your spiritual journey. A number of times these thoughts and events will unfold in what at the outset seem like very improbable coincidences. However, they are not coincidences. What happens to you is put in motion by the Holy Spirit, which knows how to tread the path home and knows what thoughts and events are helpful for guiding you along this path.

All of us living in the world live in the world because our mind is full of misperceptions. These misperceptions serve a purpose, the ego's purpose. The bigger the web of misperceptions the larger and more plentiful are the ego's lines of communication within the mind. And the harder it is to feel the gentle reminders from the Holy Spirit.

All our misperceptions seem to be fed to us by the world. However, we have been reminded that it is all in our mind and that there is not actually anything out there; there is no world out there[1]. However, our experience is not yet aligned with this. Nor will it be for as long as our mind is entwined in a web of misperceptions. So in our worldly experience, these misperceptions seem to have been made by something outside of ourselves. They seem to have been made by people and events that have touched our lives. The web of misperceptions also gives us the experience of death, like an insect experiencing death after being caught in a spider's web. While in truth there is no death, only eternal life.

One way the Holy Spirit will untangle these misperceptions is by us 'coincidentally' meeting people who will influence us in a way that makes us change our mind about something. Or we may 'coincidentally' come across a book that, after reading it, profoundly changes our mind about something. Or we may visit or revisit a place that for whatever reason we feel a mental attachment to, and making this visit changes our mind about something.

A place where I have met people who have had a positive impact on my perceptions is at workshops. One thing to remember here is that the vast majority of your perceptions are unconscious. And you may at some, often unconscious, level perceive mental wounds or attachments towards someone without actually being aware of this. There have been occasions where I have met people at workshops whom I feel I have met before. But at the same time, I know I haven't. This is often an indication of a past life connection. In that past life there may have been unresolved issues or certain misperceptions about each other. Just being in each other's energy field in this lifetime seems to on occasion have a healing effect. In general though, most people you meet, you meet because they are the ideal people to act as a catalyst for you to make helpful changes in your mind; changes that correct your perceptions toward being more aligned with the perceptions of the Holy Spirit.

In terms of books, looking back it is amazing how different

books and other written material, as well as workshops and other modes of teaching, have come into my life at just the right time to lead me step by step towards becoming ready for a non-dualistic spiritual teaching. All the teachings I have been exposed to have served a purpose. For a while, I was drawn to teachings about different dimensional existences. I seemed to have a mental attachment to these concepts. In my search for what this earthly life is all about there was probably a part of my mind that thought that what I was looking for resided in a higher dimension. So a lot of information relating to different dimensions of existence came onto my path, including the concept of ascension into the fifth dimension. Shortly after I first came across *A Course in Miracles* a visual sense about different dimensional existences came to me. It showed that living in the third dimension is like living in the basement of a house, where the air feels quite dense and there is limited lighting from the small windows close to the ceiling of the basement. Once you have ascended to the fifth dimension you have made a move up to the ground floor where the air is lighter and there is plenty of light coming in from larger windows. But you are still in the house. You are still in the ego's home. You are not *at* home. You are not free. You are still in the Illusion. You have just moved from one area of the Illusion to another. So nothing has really been achieved. Illusion is nothing, irrespective of which part of the Illusion you are in. So I realized that this must be true for all dimensions of existence. They are just different carrots used by the ego to give a sense of direction and achievement, while in truth never allowing anything to be achieved. I was looking for an answer within the Illusion Circle, expecting to find an answer where there is none. Because of my unconscious attachment to dimensional concepts, and a part of my mind trying to convince me that the answer to what I was searching for could be achieved through aiming for a higher level of consciousness, and with it higher levels of dimensional experiences, it was important for the

Holy Spirit to coax me towards looking these concepts squarely in the eye, so to speak. After doing so, I could let go of this mental attachment. This helped me to become ready for a non-dualistic spiritual teaching.

Of the more conventional spiritual books, I read Neal Donald Walsh's *Conversation with God* book series. These books seemed to help me recondition my mind as it relates to Jesus. While, despite society's attempts (in Norway the Protestant Lutheran Church was part of the state until 2012), I never became very invested in the Christian views of Jesus and the world. However, western society is so heavily influenced by Christianity that it is bound to influence people's overall belief system to some degree. The *Conversation with God* book series seemed to help me to adjust that influence as a stepping stone towards a non-dualistic belief system.

The spiritual teachings you come across that are dualistic in nature will come onto your path because there is a mental attachment that you are coaxed into letting go of in preparation for a non-dualistic spiritual teaching. The content of these dualistic teachings will be such that certain mental attachments become exposed and subsequently let go of. As you go through this process it may at times feel like you are stumbling along somewhat aimlessly. But the teachings and experiences you come across are all stepping-stones, preparing you for a higher truth. Again, there are no coincidences. Therefore, dualistic teachings play a vitally important role. There is a tendency though to become of the impression that such teachings can lead you to your goal. However, such teachings are *means* towards making you mentally ready for a non-dualistic spiritual teaching. These teachings may even present a dualistic goal as your ultimate goal, like reaching a certain level of consciousness. Be careful not to buy into such goals. The teaching that will get you to know who you are in truth will always be a non-dualistic spiritual teaching, because in truth you are non-dualistic. You are eternal spirit at one with and residing in Reality.

As far as reaching a certain level of consciousness is concerned, the term "a conscious experience" only makes sense in the Illusion. When the Illusion experience started, the mind was for the first time having a conscious experience of both self, as the ego part of the Illusion, and a conscious experience of there being something other than itself; Reality. The latter became felt as being left behind and as being outside the new ego self. In Reality there are no levels of understanding, only knowledge of all. Hence, the concept of consciousness becomes meaningless. You need two-ness, duality, or relativity in order to have the concept of consciousness. You need something else to be conscious of. Therefore, consciousness does not exist in Reality, where all is one and the same. So again, make sure not to confuse the means, which are there to help you towards your goal, with your goal. To bring about such confusion is a very successful trick in the hat of the ego. It is a great way for it to give you a sense of progress while keeping you fairly and squarely in the Illusion, exactly where the ego wants to keep you.

There are people who can achieve the goal of experiencing themselves in truth without coming across a written or spoken non-dualistic spiritual teaching. With the help of the Holy Spirit, they can discern non-dualistic truths from one or more dualistic teachings. In effect, they cherry pick non-dualistic kernels of truth from within these dualistic teachings. And through applying this truth their homecoming is achieved.

You can even gain the required non-dualistic understanding virtually entirely through self-enquiry. One ACIM student told the story of her burning inner desire to find the truth. She was inspired to seek within for truth, which she did with utmost sincerity. When she later came upon the *A Course in Miracles* material she found it very easy to understand because it articulated the understanding she had already gained through self-enquiry with what she now understands is the Holy Spirit.

When *you* are ready for a non-dualistic spiritual teaching, and a non-dualistic spiritual teaching comes across your path, it is not unusual to still feel a certain attachment to one or more of the dualistic spiritual teachings that got you to this point. I still pursued a dualistic spiritual teaching alongside my *A Course in Miracles* studies in the early days of being an ACIM student. However, this resulted in an inner conflict, and I found I was able to progress my spiritual practice faster and with greater ease once I let go of all dualistic spiritual teachings.

I have heard about similar experiences from other ACIM students. Additionally, I have heard of ACIM students who moved away from *A Course in Miracles* again, in favor of dualistic teachings. It is as though the full readiness for a non-dualistic spiritual teaching is not quite there yet. Invariably the ACIM students I have heard referencing these types of experiences have gone full circle; it has made them realize even more strongly that ACIM is a complete teaching in itself and that no other teaching is necessary. This does not mean that they are not open to listen to other teachings, they simply find that all the guidance they need towards experiencing who they are in truth is contained within the ACIM material.

Let me take a moment to point out a particular nuance to do with non-dualistic spiritual teachings that is very important. Non-dualism points to oneness. However, not all non-dualistic spiritual teachings are clear on what you are one with. Even if this is pointed out there may be inconsistencies in what they state you are one with. Some teachings will state that you are one with something in the Illusion, e.g. that the universe is one and you are one with the universe. Within the confines of the Illusion this is true. But ultimately, it cannot be the oneness that a non-dualistic spiritual teaching should point you towards, since, as has been mentioned, the Illusion isn't. Hence, nothing in the universe is either. Thus, it would be like saying that you are one with nothing. So, I want to make it abundantly clear that you are one with Reality, and nothing else; because there is nothing else. I also want to make it abundantly clear that Reality, or God or Source, did not make the Illusion. Reality has nothing to do with the Illusion and does not even know what the Illusion is. How could it? Reality knows only of perfection, of itself. Which, again, is all there is. This understanding is sometimes referred to as *pure non-dualistic spirituality*. *A Course in Miracles* is a pure non-dualistic spiritual teaching.

Because our experience is one of duality with right and wrong, good and bad, love and hate, etc., there is a tendency among some teachers of ACIM to put forth dualistic teachings in the name of ACIM. So you need to use your discernment, with the help of the Holy Spirit, to ensure that any teaching put forth about *A Course in Miracles* that you take to heart is not dualistic. It may be that you will come across a teacher mentioning *A Course in Miracles* in the context of achieving something on the level of form. With form being a concept in the Illusion, this should raise a red flag in your mind and turn your discernment on high alert[2]. And it is because this type of teaching happens that other teachers of ACIM often emphasize the non-dualistic nature of ACIM. In that context they often state that ACIM is not concerned with what happens in the world. It is only concerned with moving you towards the experience of who you are in truth; towards the experience of non-dualistic Reality.

Remember the first two Keys. *It is all in the mind* and *there is no form, only content*. This does not exactly leave room for anything to actually happen in the world.

While mentioning the world, when I first started to study ACIM I found the size of the text very daunting. Its 365 lessons; one lessen per day for one year, looked more manageable. So, against better advice (*A Course in Miracles* recommends having knowledge of the text before doing the lessons[3]), I decided to start with the workbook lessons. I figured that I had read enough spiritual books, including a couple of books about *A Course in*

d not apply to me. Once I st.
'th them pretty well. How
son I got stuck on was lesson
points out that there is no wor.
n you get to this point in th
stop and take a break from it and
time[5]. This is exactly what happened to me.
quite know why, because at a conscious level I was quite
happy to accept that there is no world. But somehow, whenever
I picked up this lesson to work on it, I just wanted to doze off. I
did not seem able to complete the lesson. Maybe it simply was
not time for me to take it any further at that time and/or maybe I
experienced too much resistance to the concept of there not being
a world at an unconscious level.

This brings up something that even baffled Sigmund Freud.
Freud had great respect for the subconscious mind but found
that even he had underestimated it. In effect, Freud healed
people by assisting them in changing their mind. Often this lead
to healing and at times it did not. Freud could have two patients
with for all intents and purposes the same need for healing. He
treated them both in the same way and one healed while the
other one did not. This was a mystery to Freud. What Freud
eventually discovered was that at a subconscious level the
person who healed wanted healing, while the person who did
not heal, while wanting healing at a conscious level, did not want
to heal at a subconscious level of his or her mind. In effect, the
subconscious was sabotaging the efforts to heal. Similarly, there
are convictions at a subconscious level of your mind that are
sabotaging your progress on your path home. These subconscious convictions are part of your web of misperceptions. It is
these subconscious convictions the Holy Spirit is here to help
you eliminate.

Therefore, do not underestimate the resistance you may feel
at an unconscious level. The more you expect and are vigilant to

stance, the greater the chance that yo
it rather than allowing the ego, or your in
the pleasure of convincing you not to keep
vard, and ultimately make it homeless. In truth, the
omeless anyway. It just thinks it is not. More importantly, it
made *you* think it is not, too. And it wants to keep it that way
Therefore, it will attempt to block your endeavors towards
achieving permanent peace of mind. So expect these resistances
and prepare yourself to work through them whenever they arise.
Because arise they will. But it is equally certain that for every
resistance that arises you will be provided with the guidance to
work through it.

In terms of visiting places, as well as feeling like going back to
a place you really like, you may also be drawn to visit a place for
no seeming reason other than you just feel you need to go there.
And once you get there it may feel like some sort of homecoming,
or you may just feel very good about being there. This may be
because of the type of energy this place contains. Or you may
have lived there before. Either way, going to a place you feel
drawn to visit may provide healing for you. And with it the need
to visit this place again may go away.

An experience of mine that comes to mind is one that relates
to a place where I used to live. It is a place in England that I have
very fond memories of, a village in London called Putney. I lived
there the last ten years prior to moving to the USA. Just over a
year after moving to the USA, we travelled back to England and
spent some time in Putney. It was great to re-connect face-to-face
with our friends there. But the experience of going to our old
haunts in Putney did not resemble my expectations of how it
would be like. The form of these places obviously did, but the
experience of going to them did not. Since then I have never felt
a need to go back to Putney. This does not mean that I do not go
back there, but there is no inner perceived need connected to the
place itself that takes me there. This example highlights the

power of mental attachment. The release of mental attachments is an important concept in *A Course in Miracles*. And let me point out here that relinquishing a mental attachment to something or someone, e.g. your best friend, does not mean that you will enjoy this 'something', or the company of your best friend, any less. If you were to relinquish your mental attachment to your best friend you would likely end up enjoying the friendship more because there would be no noise in your mind about what to expect from the friendship. You could then approach the friendship in a more natural way. And your inner peace and happiness would no longer depend on certain behaviors of your best friend. The friendship would no longer depend on your best friend fulfilling certain needs of yours. And if your best friend were to move somewhere else the grievance involved with coming to terms with this would be less painful.

None of the above examples of experiences I have had are coincidences. They are all part of what the Holy Spirit has put before me on my path in order to release certain perceptions and mental attachments that resided in my mind[6]. This clears the way for further perceptions and mental attachments to be addressed. You will have had your own unique experiences in life that fit with this perspective. For both of us though, and for everyone else for that matter, they lead us towards exactly the same goal, the goal of experiencing ourselves in truth.

I mentioned earlier that the word 'learning' should be used with care in the context of moving towards our goal of experiencing our truth. Sometimes though, you will come across references to us needing to learn lessons, references to tools of learning, and that the world is a classroom in which we learn these lessons. These are all good metaphors for moving us towards our goal. But they also have the potential of becoming a limitation in that they might give the implied impression that you do not already know everything. In truth, you are in Reality with perfect knowledge. And while your experience is of being in the Illusion, you have a memory of this knowledge stored in the part of your mind that we refer to as the Holy Spirit. You can think of the Holy Spirit as a bridge between the perception of the Illusion and the knowledge of Reality; the Holy Spirit enables perception that reflects knowledge[7].

Whenever these metaphors are used, however, it is typically also stated that you already know everything and that all you need to do is to undo what you have learned in the world. Always remember this. You are here to unlearn the story of the ego so that eventually the Holy Spirit is all that is left in your experience of the Illusion, and Reality can become your next, and last as well as only, experience. So to the extent there is anything for you to learn it is learning what is required in order to put yourself in a space of un-learning. In order to be well placed to enter this space of receptivity for un-learning it is important to know about some of the dynamics of what you aim to unlearn. Because you need to, metaphorically speaking, look at the things in your mind that you no longer want there; you need to look them in the eye and acknowledge to yourself that they are not who you are. And in that view you can let them go; release them to the Holy Spirit. In this context it is also helpful for you to learn how to improve your communication with the Holy Spirit. This will allow for the unwanted stuff in your mind to be brought to your attention in quicker succession for release. And it can make you more efficient and effective in the manner in which you release it. More on this later.

Many people have a tendency to think about adding things to their mind in connection with learning. So I would like to share with you an analogy about chipping away, with chipping away being a metaphorical description of letting go or releasing. What we are here to do is to chip away at the web of misperceptions that cloud our mind and limit our communication channel to the part of the mind that remembers Reality and can guide us home; guide us to the awareness of our oneness with Reality. This will expose the naked truth, a truth that acknowledges us as already perfect, innocent, whole and fully cared for. The Holy Spirit knows our perfection. It is coaxing us towards this understanding of ourselves, and ultimately the experience of this. So for the purpose of establishing this analogy let us equate innocence and perfection with the symbol of an angel. The Holy Spirit puts this angel in front of you and says, "This is who you are". You look at it and all you see is a block of wood. However, the Holy Spirit insists that it is an angel you are looking at. But the Holy Spirit also knows that your vision is obscured. So the Holy Spirit gives you some practical tools to clear your mind of illusory content so that your vision can be fully restored. Under the guidance of the Holy Spirit, you take these tools and start working on the outer areas of what to you seems like a block of wood. The Holy Spirit guides you to start working on the areas of the block of wood that are symbolic of your web of misperceptions, the areas that cloud your mind. Once you have followed all of its guidance you see the most beautifully carved angel standing in front of you.

As mentioned before, the ego would like you to go around in circles and not find your way home. Because once you are home, the ego becomes homeless. It has also already been mentioned that the Holy Spirit will guide you to learn lessons as they are presented. Let us now look at the latter from a different perspective. In every situation the Holy Spirit will guide you towards changing your perception of something. On this journey, all your perceptions need to be re-visited. And the guidance you receive from the Holy Spirit will lead you to opportunities for perceptions to be corrected.

Which brings us back to the concept at hand; *there are no coincidences*. Your journey will unfold in its unique way depending on the nature of the web of misperceptions in *your* mind. We will all develop our unique symbol for our communication with the Holy Spirit. For *you* it will be what suits *your* unique journey best. For a number of people the symbol is abstract like the Holy Spirit. For others a concrete symbol like Jesus or a historical being other than Jesus who has also laid aside the body for the last time works better. The symbol for communication with the Holy Spirit may evolve over time, but then again it may not. Through your chosen symbol, the Holy Spirit will always seek to provide you with opportunities that will enable *your* path to unfold effectively and gracefully.

The notion of the Holy Spirit seeking to provide opportunities for events to unfold effectively and gracefully makes me think of a meeting I had with Fran Duda a few days after I started writing this book. I learned about Fran through Carrie Triffet's book *Long Time No See*, which is a spiritual memoir about Carrie's journey of coming across *A Course in Miracles*, her years prior to this event and her first few years as an ACIM student. Beyond learning about Fran, I found Carrie's book an interesting and helpful read. It is also very humorous. Fran had helped Carrie on her journey and I felt Fran could also help me. Fran lives in Sedona. I went there to meet her.

While I was with Fran she took me to canyons and other places in and around Sedona, as she felt guided. One such place was the Loy Canyon. Fran took me to an area within the Loy Canyon where there is an old ruin up against the cliff face. Below the cliff face there is an open area that was an area dedicated to healing in former times. Fran advises in Carrie's book that she attracts wounded healers. While Fran and I were taking our first steps within the area of healing by the ruin in Loy Canyon, Fran told me that this place was a homecoming for me; not that I had necessarily lived or even been there before, but energetically it represented a homecoming for me. I felt the rising of emotions as I took these early steps within this ancient area of healing, emotions that wanted to be released. I had no concrete sense of being a wounded healer. However, I have learned a couple of energy healing modalities, and this may be linked to a need to heal an unconscious perception of being a wounded healer. In any case, as I took my early steps within the area of healing by the ruin in Loy Canyon, the sense I connected with after feeling the rising emotions was that "it is okay". As though in my web of misperceptions there were negative perceptions in connection with healing or the healing profession. It was an invitation for me to let go of these misperceptions, since in fact everything is okay. As I let these misperceptions go, I could feel my chest opening and my shoulders broadening. My spine became more erect. There was no longer a need for me to hold on to my unconscious misperceptions about healing.

After walking further along the path and arriving by the ruin set up against the cliff face, my eyes were drawn to one of the old drawings there. The drawing was of a person on his knees, with a person standing behind him with a bow and arrow. The person with the bow and arrow touched the spine with the tip of the arrow in the heart region of this person on his knees. I thought my attention was drawn to this picture as a representation of the wounded healer in me, of me being wounded by this arrow. After we left the ruin, I saw this big egg shaped rock next to the path. It was a bit taller than me and it was sliced right down the middle, with the flat side of it facing me. In front of it, between the path and this neatly sliced in two egg shaped rock, was the other half of the rock. This other half of the rock had fallen towards the path with the flat side facing up, making a horizontal platform to step onto. I felt guided to step onto it, so I did. Standing on this rock and looking back towards the ruins I found myself facing another rock of about the same height as the egg shaped rock. This rock was very narrow, a bit like a large saw wheel. And it was positioned so that it looked as though, metaphorically speaking, it could have been what had cut this egg shaped rock in two. While standing there, facing this saw wheel looking rock, I could feel a sensation in my heart region. It was as though while standing there I allowed my heart to open more widely. Just allowing my heart to open filled me with a greater degree of confidence about the road ahead. This greater opening of the heart and the resulting greater confidence also made me more relaxed. The combined effect enabled me to allow more guidance to come through from the Holy Spirit. And it came to me that the kneeling man with an arrow pointed at the heart region of his spine was a symbol of healing rather than of being wounded. And looking at the canyon as a whole, with lush vegetation at the foot of the red rock face, it seemed to symbolize what can be achieved, and what can take root, when we allow our heart to open up to the communication from the Holy Spirit.

While traveling among the canyons of Sedona, Fran told me that I had taken on ancestral guilt. And a place she felt guided to take me was a dried out watering hole with many dead fish on its dried out surface.

Well, I come from a village on an island on the west coast of Norway that up until my father's early adulthood was a thriving fishing village. My father was the third generation skipper on a fishing vessel belonging to a company founded by my great grandfather. My great grandfather skippered the first fishing vessel operated under this company. So over the three genera- tions they have caught a whole lot of fish. While my father skippered they made a catch recorded in the Guinness World of Records as 2.4 million liters of fish[8] in one catch, which equates to just over 2,300,000 kg (5,100,000 lbs). This fishing company was also fishing herring at a time when the herring stock in Norwegian waters became so depleted that they ended up with a moratorium on herring fishing lasting several years. So I guess it would not be difficult for my mind to construe some ancestral guilt regarding the killing of fish if it so wished.

I was not conscious of this guilt before meeting with Fran. But, as mentioned earlier, we are all well advised not to underestimate what might be buried in the unconscious part of our mind. I never considered it my path to take over the fishing business when my father retired. This may possibly be linked to the unconscious ancestral guilt that Fran noticed. The unconscious mind can certainly play tricks on you in all sorts of ways. One experience that comes to mind is from when I was about ten years old. I was on vacation with my family. We were visiting Frognerparken in Oslo, also called Vigeland's Park because Mr. Vigeland made all the statues that adorn the park. While there, I saw a dog playing. Somehow, during its play it hurt its mouth, which started to bleed. In my conscious mind I just observed this and thought nothing more of it. But later I started to feel dizzy and light headed and needed to sit down. I did not put two and two together at first. But eventually, I realized that seeing the dog bleeding from its mouth had made me feel faint. The trigger for this reaction was in my unconscious mind. I cannot remember experiencing this trigger before this incidence. But later, after I became consciously aware of it, I was prone to the same reaction upon seeing blood.

And this is typical of a number of our behaviors. They are like reflexes. Reflexes based on what we have "learned" while buying into the story of the ego. This is why we ultimately have to re-visit all our perceptions.

Standing by the dried out watering hole that Fran had taken me to I felt a heaviness in my heart. In this regard, I would like to mention that when you feel emotional pain, and feel guided by the Holy Spirit to release the related mental attachments, it is not important for you to know what gave rise to this emotional pain. In this particular instance I knew I felt the heaviness in my heart because Fran had told me about guilt related to my family heritage of killing fish. Whether or not *you* know the reason for the emotional pain in a given situation, you are always advised to seek the help of the Holy Spirit to chip away at the misperceptions in your mind that cause you emotional pain. In the process of doing so, the reason for the emotional pain may or may not come to mind. But whether it does or not, the chipping away at your web of misperceptions will still take place; it is this that ultimately is important. For example, I did not know the reason why I had emotional wounds in connection with healing, but I was still able to release it while in Loy Canyon.

I mentioned earlier that it is a requirement to look the thought system of the ego in the eye as part of your release from it. Let me use this opportunity to point out that you only need to recognize and acknowledge in your mind that the reason for an emotional pain is **the thought system of the ego**. It does not need to be any more specific than this. The emotional pain is symbolic of the web of misperceptions in your mind, ultimately rooted in the original guilt and fear. It is not a part of who you are in truth. You do not need to look at the specific underlying reasons that gave you an emotional pain. Again, all you need to do is acknowledge the emotional pain and with it acknowledge that it comes from the ego, and that the ego is not who you are. Then, release it to the Holy Spirit.

However, there may be times when knowing what underlies the emotional pain will be helpful for further chipping away at the web of misperceptions. When this is the case the Holy Spirit will provide you with a sense of what this underlying reason for the emotional pain is.

When, in my mind, I sought guidance from the Holy Spirit while at the dried out watering hole with many dead fish on its dried out surface, the message I connected with was a poignant one. I was at this watering hole shortly after the end of the rainy season. And the watering hole was already dry. Normally it does not dry out until about eight months after the rainy season. The symbolism of this gave me the message loud and clear. If nature wants to deplete fishing resources, or replenish them for that matter, it does not need the help of man. It is more than capable of doing it itself. I realized then that I did not have to worry about any fishing done by my ancestors, or anyone else. Through this sense, I was given the opportunity to release the ancestral guilt I had about catching fish on a large scale.

Let us be careful here and not start equating the way the Holy Spirit thinks with the way our conscious mind tends to think. Remember, the Holy Spirit is not concerned with what happens in the world. However, rest assured that the Holy Spirit will ensure that helpful opportunities to move you along your path will always be provided. So do not take the message I sensed to mean that any killing of fish is okay. Messages from the Holy Spirit are often highly personalized. The message I connected with at the watering hole was such a highly personalized message. And it achieved its objective of me allowing myself to release my ancestral guilt to the Holy Spirit.

It is also because of this often highly personalized communication between you and the Holy Spirit that two people may read the same spiritual book, or listen to the same spiritual talk, and get very different personal takeaways from it. Everything that happens in life, whether it is exposure to a spiritual book or talk, or something else you connect with in life, it is an opportunity for the Holy Spirit to communicate to you. And the communication you pick up is what is the most appropriate for you at that point on your journey. So be careful with the generalization of the messages you receive. It may be perfect for you but that does not necessarily mean that it is also perfect for another. Again, these are synchronicities at play in order to help *you* along *your* path.

This also brings up another important point. To tell others what to do is not your job. Nor is it your job to focus on how others need to change. More likely than not, dabbling in these activities is a decoy tactic of the ego. It becomes a distraction away from focusing on yourself and your own path.

It may be useful from time to time to remind ourselves that the message of *A Course in Miracles* reflects the message Jesus gave while he walked the earth. It is just presented differently. Partly because a typical mindset among the readers of ACIM is in many ways different to a typical mindset of the people Jesus addressed at that time. Also, there is not the same need to worry about blasphemy these days. Most people did not fully get Jesus' message at the time. Equally, most people are not ready for the message put forth in *A Course in Miracles* today. Synchronicities will connect the people who are ready for its message to *A Course in Miracles*, either directly or via literature about it. Even though the final destination is the same for everyone, the path to it is not. And for some a teaching other than ACIM is a more helpful guide to this destination; an experience of who they are in truth. But since you are reading this book, odds are that the message presented in *A Course in Miracles* is helpful to you, and that you are ready for it. So, sticking with the fish theme, I will ask a question related to one of the sayings in the Gospel of Thomas. "If you were a fisherman with a catch of many small fish and one big fish, what would you do with *your* catch?"[9]

This brings us to the next Key: "there are always only two choices".

Exercise

Before we move on to the next Key, let's again bring a new exercise into your life. We have asserted that *there are no coincidences*. So going forward, catch those happenings in your life that you would normally consider a coincidence, and revisit your perception about each of those events. Could it be that they all happen for a reason, and that in seeing that they happen for a reason you can gain further insights into which of your misperceptions are ready for correction? Furthermore, do they provide insights about the nature of your path towards experiencing yourself in truth? Allow for the correction of your mind and/or take action, accordingly.

In my experience, the more mindful I am about the non-coincidental, or synchronistic, nature of what happens in my life the more synchronistic events come into my life. This could simply be a matter of me being more mindful of their occurrence, or it could point to a speeding up along my path; a speeding up that calls for the need for a quicker succession of synchronicities to take place.

Chapter 5

There are Always Only Two Choices

So, the fourth Key is: **There are always only two choices**. This is not to say that it does not seem like we have a multitude of choice. A multitude of choice is indeed our experience. But then again, that is what the ego is all about, separation and multiplicity. The ego has taken the one mind and scattered it into a near infinite number of pieces, generally referred to as the universe. And as well as giving us the impression that we are victims and can ascribe all our problems and issues to others through projection, it also gives us the impression of a lot of choice. But all of its presented choices are still a choice of choosing with the ego, which is a choice of nothing. A pretend choice that will keep you firmly stuck in the Illusion of time and space. The alternative is the choice presented by the Holy Spirit, a choice that will eventually uncover your true self, and allow you to leave this Illusion behind. These are your only two choices[1].

Let's first look at who the "you" is who chooses between the ego and the Holy Spirit. Who is this "you"? This "you" is the split mind as a whole. Remember the first Key, *it is all in the mind*. Hence, the "you" in the Illusion is in the split mind. You, in the split mind, always choose between aligning with the ego part of the split mind or the Holy Spirit part of the split mind. By choosing one, you give up the other[2]. And you can always choose again. So if you find yourself aligned with the ego, you can choose in any moment to instead align with the Holy Spirit.

Which takes us back to the question: "if you were a fisherman with a catch of many small fish and one big fish, what would you do with your catch?" The many small fish represent the many choices presented by the ego, which take you on a merry-go-round within the Illusion[3]. The big fish represents choosing with the Holy Spirit, and as such invites you to be guided to your experience of Reality; your true home, who you are in truth. Your time of choosing is at hand.

While the Holy Spirit had my attention at the watering hole it also took the opportunity to deepen my understanding of this concept. As the water in this watering hole had dried out it had left a white imprint, as though it was colored with white chalk. This imprint had the shape of a large fish. Within and around this imprint was where all the small dead fish were lying. The white fish imprint looked kind of otherworldly. It somehow seemed to be in control of its destiny, being able to turn up wherever it could act as a communication tool. Not like the dead fish which seemed to be tossed around at the whim of the ego. The dead fish seemed to mirror the ego's wish to control every- thing while in reality being unable to control anything. All the while the Holy Spirit is in full control, and can therefore be fully trusted. We just have to allow it to do its miracle work. It will never impose itself on us. But it always responds to our invitation, albeit often not in the way our mainly ego controlled mind expects it to respond. So always aim to keep an open heart and mind. Allow grace to make miracles unfold. Again, be reminded that *it is all in the mind*. The Holy Spirit is not concerned with what happens in the world, but rather with enabling your path to unfold in the most helpful way on your journey home. As part of this your perception of the world will change and often there will also be some bi-products in the form of tangible changes in the world.

This is a good place to stop and look at what a miracle is. What is a miracle? And how does a miracle happen? A miracle is something that manifests due to a change in your mind; a change in your mind due to it having had some of the web of mispercep- tions chipped away[4]. We typically tend to think of a miracle as something that happens in the world. But such a miracle is always *caused* by a change of perception in the mind. This is important to understand. So let me also put it the other way around. A change of perception in the mind is always the cause of a miracle.

There are times when we have a temporary change of mind, which results in a temporary miracle. Once we revert to our earlier frame of mind, the miracle ceases. The story in the New Testament of Peter walking on water with Jesus illustrates this. Jesus knew perfectly well that the world is an illusion. With the Holy Spirit, he could transcend the laws of the world. So being aligned with the Holy Spirit he could walk on water as a means of teaching others. With us all being of the one mind and there being one Holy Spirit, Jesus was able to connect with Peter through the Holy Spirit. And Peter became of the mind that he could also walk on water. So he did. But then the ego regained Peter's attention by encouraging him to focus his attention on the strong wind and the waves. At this point Peter started to sink.

This story also illustrates that the Holy Spirit does not force anything on you[5]. And its voice is as loud as your willingness to listen[6]. Peter first chose to listen to and follow the Holy Spirit alongside Jesus. He subsequently chose to side with the part of his mind in which the ego resides. This is in effect what free will is. Free will is your freedom to choose with the ego or with the Holy Spirit. Again, it may seem like the ego presents many choices. But these choices are all the same in their nothingness, and in that they either solidify or increase the web of misperceptions. Choosing with the Holy Spirit, on the other hand, diminishes the web of misperceptions in the mind. So there are no neutral thoughts[7]. A thought on the one hand either solidifies or increases the web of misperceptions or, on the other hand, it diminishes the web of misperceptions.

As a last point on miracles, I would like to stress before we move on that the miracle should not be your focus[8]. The miracle is something that naturally happens because you apply this teaching[9]; it gives you experiences you otherwise would not have, experiences of moving along your path towards knowing yourself in truth. But these experiences, these miracles, are tools to help and/or encourage you along your journey. It can be tempting to focus on the wish for certain miracles to take place, but that would be misplaced focus. Your focus is better placed on your end goal. If you expect certain miracles to happen along the way, and they don't, you open up for an opportunity to think with the ego that you must be doing something wrong. But if you keep your focus on your goal you will connect with the right opportunities for continued progress along your path.

In our daily experience there seem to be a lot of luring choices. And they somehow seem to speak to us quite loudly so that our attention is assured. There are bills to be paid, there is work to be done, there are physical objects we aspire to have, and there are societal expectations that we feel we need to comply with. The list can at times seem endless. And the emotions these items give rise to, which is often some level of emotional pain around what it would mean *not* to comply with these "demands", often leaves little space for inner self reflection and peace. And it is in moments of inner self reflection that we often are most receptive to catch the gentle nudges from the Holy Spirit.

By following your intuition you can make great progress. And while making progress on your path home can seem at odds with what your ego makes you think you want to achieve in life, let me remind you of what the late Steve Jobs, co-founder of Apple, once said; "Your time is limited, so don't waste it living someone else's life. Don't be trapped by dogma - which is living with the results of other people's thinking. Don't let the noise of other's opinions drown out your own inner voice. And most importantly, have the courage to follow your heart and intuition. They somehow already know what you truly want [...]. Everything else is secondary."

At this point I would like to say something about how to perceive the Holy Spirit. There is a tendency to think in terms of higher wisdom. This may be a way of thinking about it that works for you. In my practice of connecting with the Holy Spirit I like to get away from ego concepts. One of the concepts of the ego is hierarchy. There are typically different levels of things, like big houses and small houses, big cars and small cars, fast cars and slow cars, nice neighborhoods and neighborhoods to be avoided. The ego loves classification. Higher and lower wisdom is just one more of these classifications. It is difficult to move away from a directional perspective entirely though. The perspective I feel best represents the oneness of who we are and the experience of connecting with the Holy Spirit is **inner wisdom**, or **inner guidance**. This firmly acknowledges that this wisdom or guidance resides inside of us, leaving very little room for perceiving that it resides with some higher power somewhere out there or up there.

On the topic of aligning yourself with the Holy Spirit, how can you start to improve your connection with the Holy Spirit, or your inner wisdom and guidance? The end of chapter exercises help you with this. Beyond the exercises, the most obvious would be to start by paying more attention to your intuition or gut feeling. Intuition and gut feeling are typically communication from the Holy Spirit. And at the point when you realize that you have just had an intuitive thought you often feel a warm feeling in your heart region, or you may feel a shiver down your spine. Over time, you will learn what *your* feelings around these intuitions are, and increasingly learn to trust them. One word of caution though, the ego is prone to start planting thoughts of doubt into your mind at this point. Because the last thing the ego wants is for you to increase your trust in, and strengthen your communication with, the Holy Spirit. Don't listen to these doubts. Stay firm in your trust of your intuition and don't give the ego the pleasure of continuing to stall you on your path.

Let me also point out that it is one thing to have achieved a greater *ability* to receive communication from the Holy Spirit and it is another to consciously align yourself with this communication. Prior to meeting with Fran I had already made progress regarding my ability to receive communication from the Holy Spirit. But I was largely failing in consciously aligning myself with the communication from the Holy Spirit.

Always remember that whether you choose to listen to the Holy Spirit is your choice; you are the boss. You are in charge. You decide between the two choices of the ego and the Holy Spirit; you decide whether you want to align with the voice of the Holy Spirit and whether you want to follow its nudges. The Holy Spirit will not force anything onto you[10]. It is a bit like you are the boss and the Holy Spirit is one of your subordinates whom you may or may not choose to listen to and whose advise you may or may not choose to heed. Think of it as you being the boss sitting in an office with a door leading onto the work floor. You can choose to leave the door open or you can choose to close it. However, the door is never locked. So either way there is a way for your subordinates to come and talk to you. With your door closed, they are less likely to do so. But with the door open, they can feel free to do so whenever they feel the need. It is similar with the Holy Spirit. If you keep the communication channel door shut you are less likely to pick up communication, irrespective of your *ability* to do so. If you keep it open, by being intent on aligning yourself with the Holy Spirit, you are more likely to consciously notice these communications.

In order to improve your connection with the Holy Spirit you can also make use of your understanding of how the ego works. One thing you have learned about the ego is that it uses projection, and how you see and interpret what you project becomes your perception of reality. What this means in practice is that what grabs your attention and generates feelings in you about other people or events is a mirror of what you have projected. And you project it because you do not feel comfortable with taking ownership of this issue. With a bit of self inquiry, by this concept alone you will probably learn a thing or two about yourself and which thoughts in your mind would be helpful to release to the Holy Spirit for correction, rather than continuing the recycling process of projection. Maybe ask yourself; what presses my buttons? What situations tend to upset me?

You also see what you believe. This is the same dynamic at work. The world is such a rich tapestry that whatever you believe can be reflected back at you. Your reflected reality is a function of your perception. As your perception changes the tapestry of the world starts to reflect something else back to you. For example, before you may have seen a politician on TV and thought of him or her as aggressive and lacking in compassion. After a change in your perception you may start to see the same politician as needy and craving love, attention and recognition. You are looking at exactly the same thing. The only thing that has changed is your perception of what you see. Observing your changes in perception, which are miracles, is often a good indicator of the progress you are making along your path.

One of the neat things with this is that as well as seeing how your perception plays itself out in your mind you can recognize the alternative perception of someone who has not worked on chipping away at their misperceptions. They are yet to experience your perception. If you sense that they are ready for this alternative perception, you may try to introduce it to them. But because their belief system is currently disharmonious with this alternative perception, you may have a hard time getting them to see it. Depending on how ready and open they are for it, it may or may not be in their best interest for you to try to explain it to them.

The Holy Spirit and your interaction with it works a bit like that. The Holy Spirit has seen everything you have seen. And it is aware of all the corrections of your perceptions that are required in order for you to re-gain your experience of who you are in truth. Hence, the Holy Spirit will always know your current perception of something, and it knows the next evolutionary step in your perceptual development, so to speak, and will present this to you via a lesson. This lesson can take one of many forms. It may be through an interaction with someone, something you read, something you watch on TV, or any other event that triggers you to question your current perception. The Holy Spirit will only present something to you if you are ready for it. However, since this will be a new perspective for you, you may resist it. The resistance you feel is of the ego, and the web of misperceptions it has made in your mind. If you sense a resistance, the Holy Spirit invites you to hand your resistance over to it. This is an invitation to allow the Holy Spirit to chip away the misperception that generates this resistance in your mind. As mentioned in the previous chapter, it can be helpful to release this resistance to the Holy Spirit after first acknowledging that the resistance is of the ego, and further acknowledging that the ego is not who you are. You are in Reality. It may also be helpful to keep the mental picture presented in Chapter 1 of the Reality and Illusion Circles in your mind while you acknowledge this.

The easiest way for most people to connect with the Holy Spirit is through meditation or some other form of quiet time. While in this state of mind, you can set the intention of connecting with this part of your mind that remembers, or can look into, Reality. For a lot of people it is easier to achieve this through a concrete symbol, like Jesus or another historical person who achieved a permanent experience of who they are in truth. For me the more abstract term Holy Spirit works best. I do not know why I connect the most with the term Holy Spirit. But once I realized that I do I did not question it. I simply accepted that this was the most useful symbol for me. However, more recently, there are situations where Jesus is the symbol I gravitate towards. *A Course in Miracles* mainly uses the Holy Spirit, but also Jesus, as a symbol for this part of your memory. For some of you it will be obvious what your choice of symbol is. For others it will not be quite so obvious. If it is not obvious for you just spend some time enjoying experimenting with it. While doing this you may even find that you catch a certain feeling of peace and connectedness. When you catch this feeling, you know you have made a connection with the Holy Spirit. This sometimes happens to me. I sometimes end up bypassing any mental reference to the Holy Spirit or Jesus and go straight to the *feeling* of this connection with the Holy Spirit.

Since it is typically easier to connect with the Holy Spirit while you are on your own with your own thoughts than while interacting with others, do not start to get concerned if you find it difficult to gain insights from this inner wisdom and guidance while in the company of others. If you pick up some communication from the Holy Spirit while with others then that is great. If not, then that is great too. You may find though that later while you are quiet with your own thoughts your mind might become mindful of certain interactions with people earlier that day. This would be one way for the Holy Spirit to communicate with you about it after the event rather than during it. Either way is good. Any communication with the Holy Spirit is a positive thing. And all communication is an invitation to revisit a perception and hand it over to the Holy Spirit for correction, or change, towards the Holy Spirit's perception. Such a change of perception, or change of mind, is a miracle. From the perspective of the second Key, *there is no form, only content,* this change of perception is towards content, the content of unconditional love, and away from form.

As mentioned before, you will come up against inner resistance as you progress along your path home. The web of misperceptions in your conscious as well as your subconscious mind causes this inner resistance. You may find that in your conscious mind you are happy to accept and embrace certain new concepts.

Like when I first embarked on lesson 132 in the *A Course in Miracles* workbook. I did not feel at a conscious level that I had an issue with the concept of there not being a world. But I clearly did at a subconscious level, outside of my conscious awareness. And the subconscious has a very strong hold on you. Often it is too strong for your conscious mind to override it. But that is okay. If that is how it is then that is how it is. There is a way around it though. It may take a bit of patience, but it works. And the way around it is to choose with the Holy Spirit in situations and people interactions that arise; maybe by mentally seeing the common thread connecting you and all people with the Holy Spirit. Or, you may choose to see the loving oneness of all people through their connection with the Holy Spirit. And then acknowledge that you are not separate from these people, nor are you the one having the thoughts that bear witness to such separation. Those thoughts are of the ego. You are not that, rather you and all others are in truth in Reality. And you hand the ego thoughts of separation over to the Holy Spirit. By aligning with the perspective of the Holy Spirit in this way, you will automatically chip away at the web of misperceptions in your mind that made these resistances, whether these resistances reside in your conscious or subconscious mind. There will come a time when the misperception in your mind that earlier had generated a too strong resistance for you will have been chipped away. And you can now move through this issue that you earlier had a too strong resistance to work through. This is what happened to me between my first and second encounter with this lesson 132 in the workbook. Whatever misperceptions I had in my subconscious mind generating the resistance I experienced the first time around had been chipped away by the time I got to this same lesson the second time, allowing me to work through the lesson successfully.

This also brings up the issue of want versus willingness. There may be a number of things you want to do or have. But the list of things you are willing to pursue through to accomplishment is a lot shorter. This is because for most of your 'wants' there is a resistance to do what it takes to accomplish it. To move from 'want' to 'willingness' is a function of overcoming the resistance in your mind to do what it takes to accomplish what you want or, on occasion, to realize that you don't want it after all. The first step in this process is to chip away at the misperceptions that generate the resistance. You will often not consciously know what these misperceptions are. But the Holy Spirit knows what they are and can make use of the tapestry of the world to give you the experiences you need in order to correct these misperceptions, or otherwise change your mind in a more direct way by inspiring certain profound thoughts. So again, by aligning yourself with the choice of the Holy Spirit, grace will come into your life allowing you to work through whichever obstacles are on your path home.

This Key, *there are always only two choices*, asks us to develop a willingness to choose with the Holy Spirit. It asks us to lay aside what we ordinarily think of as our own choices, choices we now understand are predominantly rooted in the ego, and instead choose with the Holy Spirit; choose with the part of us that is detached from our personality and our individuality. I have come across teachers of ACIM who want to avoid or skirt around the issue of highlighting that we want the Holy Spirit to take decisions for us rather than making them ourselves, as though this thought is too scary and/or too off-putting to mention. In my experience it has been immensely helpful to have been reminded of this relatively early on. Without this reminder I feel I would have been prone to study the ACIM text with the ego more, and even more so be prone to practice its teaching with the ego as my primary guide.

Starting to realize that we are encouraged to make decisions with the Holy Spirit, and as such disengage the ego part of us, disengage the part of us that we have nurtured and developed for our whole lives, can be hard to swallow at first. Or we may be okay with it at an intellectual level, like I was okay with there not being a world at an intellectual level, while at the same time I felt resistance towards it in everyday life's presented situations. This is okay; this is how it is for most people. However, it is still helpful to set that stake in the ground, making it clearer in our mind that making our decisions with the Holy Spirit is one of the things we are aiming for along the path to our goal of experiencing ourselves in truth. This allows us to set this as a clear intention and develop a real willingness to achieve it. And as we go about our work of chipping away at the web of misperceptions, the resistances that stand in our way of achieving it will over time ebb away. There is no way they cannot. And the time will come when handing your decisions over to the Holy Spirit is no longer only your intellectual preference, but also your daily choice.

Be open minded in terms of how the Holy Spirit will communicate with you. The more open minded you are about its channels of communication the more the Holy Spirit will use them. If you are open to receive messages in your dreams, you will pick up messages in your dreams. You may be drawn to a certain lyric. When you listen closely to this lyric, it may answer a question on your mind, or it may help shift your perception about something. When I was heading back home after my visit with Fran, I walked past a shop at the airport where they sold "Life is good" merchandise. Within minutes of passing this shop, I saw an advert for a cruise vacation. Part of the text on the advert stood out: "catch the fun". So the overall message was "Life is good, catch the fun".

While with Fran I mentioned to her that often I do not feel at home on earth. I sometimes feel this. These types of thoughts should be seen as warning signs though. It is an ego play that generally achieves two things. It makes my thoughts heavy and it directs my attention outside of myself. No answer lies outside of myself[11]. And heavy thoughts lead to a closed mind, leaving little space for communication from the Holy Spirit. So the message I received at the airport was very apt, leaving me in a more positive and lighter frame of mind.

The message at the airport also helped emphasize something else. Some students of *A Course in Miracles* can at times be prone to think of life in the world as a bit of a drag. To some, having to go through all of what life entails just to unlearn all our misperceptions can seem a bit depressing at times. I have had these thoughts. However, again, only the ego is served by these thoughts. And by aligning your thoughts with the ego your earthly pursuits will end up dragging on longer still. So a change in perception away from it being a drag to it being a good life where we have ample opportunity to catch the fun is not only more uplifting, but it will also get you home faster.

But let us not forget the many benefits of aligning ourselves with the Holy Spirit. As one example, earlier in my life I felt I had to chase things I wanted in life. Now, by following the guidance of the Holy Spirit, more often than not, things kind of come to me or somehow just come into my life. So the rewards for applying these Keys are significant. The need for mental discipline will not go away, although it becomes easier with practice. But to the extent that it feels like hardship, in my experience this hardship is a lot less than the hardship of an approach to life where I feel in control while my life is actually at the whim of circumstances concocted by the ego. And the last thing the ego wants is for me to get a taste of home. The ego wants me to keep regurgitating what it considers to be its masterpiece, through projecting my unwanted issues rather than releasing and letting them go.

It might be useful here to remind ourselves that there is only one mind. And there is only one ego, appearing as many. Each seeming individual person with its seeming individual ego is projecting different aspects of this one ego mind onto the world. The aggregate of what seems to be manifesting out in the world is a picture of the one mind's inner condition[12]. As an individual you are harboring some of these inner conditions. This is through choice. It is through the choice of listening to the voice of the ego. You can now choose to listen to the voice of the Holy Spirit, and through doing so gain an inner condition of ever diminishing misperceptions. And your experiences in the world will reflect this. You will become naturally more understanding towards people and their situation. The same goes for events you see taking place in the world, including events that directly affect you. Having less of a web of misperceptions clouding your mind allows you to see things from a different perspective, a perspective that is increasingly aligned with the loving perspective of the Holy Spirit.

One thing you will find as you practice aligning with the Holy Spirit is that in any given situation it is impossible to align with both the ego and the Holy Spirit at the same time. An example that comes to mind is in my role as a parent. I love my two girls. But I also get angry with them at times. What I find is that when I feel anger towards one of the girls I am, in that moment of feeling anger, unable to connect with my love for her. Equally, while my mind is filled with my love for them I am unable to feel anger towards them.

If you think about it, the inner feeling that accompanies anger is one of righteousness, which is a form of judgment[13]. With the other person being considered to be in the wrong, a conflict is perceived, and with it a sense of separation. And also a sense of specialness, since I see myself in the right and the other person in the wrong. All of which are typical attributes of the ego thought system.

In our obscured beliefs in our ego dominated mind we tend to be led to believe that anger and love go hand in hand. This belief even spills over into religions. But, through *A Course in Miracles*, the Holy Spirit tells us differently[14]. And my experience with my daughters demonstrates experientially that the two do *not* go together.

Talking of experiences, it is possible to have an experience of Reality while your general experience otherwise is one of being in the Illusion. Again, the two experiences cannot happen at the same moment in time. Rather, your experience is momentarily of Reality rather than of the Illusion. *A Course in Miracles* refers to this as Revelation. This experience gives you a taste of what your permanent experience will be once you regain a permanent experience of Reality only. People who have had this experience, and from whom I have had the pleasure of hearing and/or reading about it, have all been in awe of it. And it has increased their determination to align with and choose with the Holy Spirit.

This brings us nicely to the next Key: "it is about the experience, not the theory".

Exercise

We have talked a lot about connecting with communication from the Holy Spirit in this chapter. In life, be mindful of ways in which the Holy Spirit may try to communicate with you, whether this is during a quiet time or meditation, through music, a book or something else your attention is drawn towards. Be mindful that *there are always only two choices*, and make a sincere effort to choose in accordance with inspirations from the Holy Spirit. Work on trusting this guidance, even though it may seem naïve at first to do so. The ego will certainly try to convince you, through a level of doubt about your Holy Spirit communication experience, that you would be a fool to follow such guidance, a fool to think that it comes from the wisdom of your right mind. However, by sticking with this practice, over time you will learn to truly trust this guidance, and there will no longer be a sense of it being naïve to trust it. Make a mental or written note of Holy Spirit communications and, where applicable, your experience from following its guidance.

Chapter 6

It is About the Experience, Not the Theory

So, the fifth Key is: **it is about the experience, not the theory**.

There is only one ultimate truth. How else can it be the ultimate truth? This book is not about the ultimate truth. The ultimate truth cannot be captured by symbols like the written word. The written word can only point you toward the ultimate truth. The ultimate truth needs to be experienced. The experience of Reality; Revelation, referred to at the end of the previous chapter, is a taste of the experience of the ultimate truth.

Your everyday experiences are a bit like your progress report card. They are your evidence that changes have taken place in your mind. So your experiences can be one of your motivators. The way ahead may look long and daunting at times, but by focusing on how you experience life today versus how your life seemed to you, say, six or twelve months ago, you are more likely to feel that the glass is half full rather than half empty. So take the time every now and again to take stock of how you perceive and experience life now versus at some point in your past.

There may be times when you feel you're in a deep valley. For some people there will be some dark moments while they go through some of their deeper and stronger resistances. And this may happen to you. So there may be times when you have to go on virtually pure trust and faith. And looking back at *experiences* you have had earlier on your journey can give you that trust and faith. Just know that if you were to have this type of difficult experience it is a sign that you *are* ready to work through it. The experience would not be presented to you unless you were ready for it. When you get to the other side of the experience you will be glad you persevered and worked through it.

I mention this here because after following the guidance

given by the first four Keys some of you might already have come up against strong resistances. For some of you this will never happen to any major degree. It has not happened in a big way to me, so I do not have any firsthand experience I can relay to you. The closest experience to this of mine that comes to mind is a powerful ego experience I had when I first started my meditation practice. I had been to a retreat, which included an introduction to meditation. I got on with it quite well for a beginner, and I enjoyed the experience of it. I also got to know a person there who had had a daily meditation practice for just over a year. This seemed to have done wonders for her. She seemed so calm, peaceful and together, something she informed me had not always been the case.

I wanted some more of those qualities, so I decided to start my own daily meditation practice. I started to meditate in the mornings before work. While my meditation experiences had been pleasant during the retreat, and often still were in my own practice at home, some meditations were not. They were in fact the complete opposite; they were very unpleasant. A strange sensation came over my mouth, tongue and upper chest area. The most prominent sensation was in my tongue. It felt swollen and seemed to take on an alien consistency. And the saliva in my mouth took on a strange taste. My mouth went a bit numb and my upper chest area experienced a slight contraction.

It was very uncomfortable and unnerving, especially since I recognized this experience. I had had it once before, while having a very high temperature at around the age of ten. Back then, the next thing I knew I was delirious. I behaved like a possessed mad man. I was fully aware of everything I was doing but I was not in control of it. And the memory of it has stayed with me since. So to put it mildly, experiencing these sensations again, while in meditation, made me feel very uncomfortable. But in meditation I still retained a lot of control, and felt sure I could avoid it getting out of hand. It also started to dawn on me what was happening. I realized there was a part of me that was uncomfortable with me starting a meditation practice. When I had a high temperature this part of me was probably worried about my well-being. Maybe it thought I could die. Now, while in meditation, it seemed like this part of me, which generated these sensations, was getting worried that this could be the end of its cozy unquestioned existence; maybe even the beginning of its annihilation. So I stayed with these feelings as detached as I could, and eventually they subsided. This experience happened to me during a number of my earlier meditations. But I learned to handle it and it never got the better of me.

Since you have had the courage to move on to this chapter, let us get into the crux of what this concept is all about. I like what Gary Renard said about *A Course in Miracles* in a workshop I attended: **it is not about what it is about**. This captures the point well. As a student of ACIM my aim is not to have perfect knowledge of every theoretical aspect of ACIM. My aim as a student of ACIM is to allow myself to develop an understanding that will enable me to open up and communicate with the Holy Spirit and to receive guidance towards the experience of who I am in truth. While an understanding of the Keys is important, it is not enough in order to get me home. It is the application of the Keys, and the experiences I have as a result of applying the Keys, which will get me home. These experiences will enable me to develop an ever-stronger relationship with the Holy Spirit. This allows for ever more highly personalized input into this journey of mine. As part of this the Holy Spirit will sometimes direct me towards reading passages in *A Course in Miracles* that are apt for my next level of chipping away at the web of misperceptions. At other times, it will direct me to other literature or written material. Many times it is through people I meet and interact with, or situations I encounter, that act as catalysts for a new awareness about my ego thought system, and the related need for a shift in my perception. Or I may simply receive inspired thoughts. As I follow the direction given, my web of misperceptions is increasingly eroded.

There are a few experiences I have had leading up to writing this book, and while writing it, that might be useful to share. It will illustrate some of the ways in which the Holy Spirit communication has worked in my life. There are a few elements to the story so bear with me. As I have already mentioned, I learned about Fran Duda through Carrie Triffet's book *Long Time No See*. I have read this book twice. The first time I read it I found the descriptions of Carrie's meetings with Fran fascinating. But I was left with no sense or feeling that I wanted to make an appointment with Fran. As far as the overall book goes I really enjoyed it and recommended it to my wife. My wife started reading it but quickly felt it was not for her. Then some months later, she felt she should read it after all. When my wife then read the book she really enjoyed it and connected with it. She also felt she wanted to make an appointment with Fran. With my wife having enjoyed the read so much, and her excitement about the sections involving Fran, I experienced a wish to read the book again. So I did. It was while reading it this second time that I experienced shivers down my spine when I read that Fran attracts wounded healers. And I started to feel that I should make an appointment with Fran. As I felt more into it with the Holy Spirit, I sensed that I should make a one-on-one appointment, rather than a joint one with my wife. And that the timing would be in two to three months' time.

During my first read of Carrie's book, it didn't even register that Fran attracted wounded healers. It was clearly not time for me to deal with this issue at that point. But when I felt guided to read the book for a second time, the time to do so was at hand. Within three months of reading the book for a second time, I was on my way to my appointment with Fran. And one week before the appointment I started to receive strong messages, mainly in my dreams, that it was time to start writing this book. I started writing the book on a Tuesday and on the following Saturday I had my appointment with Fran.

I found that a little earlier I had connected with seven key concepts, or Keys. I now realized that these seven Keys were meant to form the backbone of this book. However, I had limited concrete ideas about the content to put in the book in connection with these seven Keys. In general, I found it difficult to connect with the Holy Spirit as far as the specific content for this book was concerned. But the healings I had experienced while with Fran meant that I was now better at opening up to communication from the Holy Spirit. And the relevant content came when I needed it. On occasion the Holy Spirit still needed help to get the content through to me though. Sometimes it used my wife. At times Lucy would say something that triggered a thought regarding content for the book. At other times my mind's attention was drawn to something outside of me, which then acted as a trigger for content.

Today, when I started writing this chapter, I had next to no prior idea about its content. 90 plus percent of the communication about its content has come while writing it. [NOTE: *These are not word communications. They are more a sense of the type of content to be included.*] When I finished the fourth paragraph of this chapter I thought to myself that it sounded a bit on the downbeat side. But I guess some of you have already experienced strong resistance the Keys presented so far.

We have been reminded that the Holy Spirit sees us all as perfect and as pure love. While we know this intellectually, take care not to try to exhibit these qualities at the expense of being true to your feelings; because right now you do not have the experience of being perfect and pure love. If you did, you would not be here in the world. The reason why you are here in the world in the first place is *because* you have bought into the ego story of misperceptions. So rather than expecting to be able to be perfect just because you are now aligning yourself more with the part of your mind where the Holy Spirit resides, try instead to notice where you feel resistance towards following the nudges of the Holy Spirit. The experience of these resistances tells you that there is a misperception in your mind blocking you from being receptive to the Holy Spirit's nudges. Mentally acknowledge this to yourself, while at the same time acknowledge that that resistance is not you. You are in truth in Reality. Then hand this resistance over to the Holy Spirit for your misperception to be corrected. This correction of your mind will then be taken care of by the Holy Spirit. It knows what to do. It is a bit like your various bodily functions of the heart, lungs, digestive system, etc. They all know what to do without your conscious input. Just mentally release the resistance to the Holy Spirit and trust its ability to correct your mind in the same way that you trust a healthy bodily function to perform its assigned role.

Meditation is a good way to experience and nurture your connection with the Holy Spirit. So let me share two alternative meditations with you. The first can be used for an abstract symbol of the Holy Spirit as well as with a concrete symbol like Jesus. The second works for a concrete symbol like Jesus only.

Firstly, get yourself seated in a comfortable position. This is the first meditation:

Close your eyes and set the intention to connect with the Holy Spirit*. Notice any thoughts that arise that are not of the Holy Spirit, thoughts that are not gentle and loving. Whenever such thoughts arise, refrain from judging them in any way. Do not entertain these thoughts. Simply acknowledge their presence and further acknowledge that these thoughts are not who you are. Then, in your mind, hand these thoughts over to the Holy Spirit and let them go; let them float by. Do this for every thought that surfaces. Thereafter, just sit in silence as you experience your connection with the Holy Spirit. Do not expect anything to happen as such. Just enjoy the experience of peace, love, calmness and connectedness.

*Use whatever symbol works best for you, e.g. Jesus or the Holy Spirit, while setting this intention.

This is the second meditation:

Close your eyes. In your mind's eye, see Jesus* in the distance. He is walking towards you. He comes up to you and he smiles warmly. He then embraces you and gives you a kiss on the forehead. Feel the loving warmth of his presence. Next, mentally prepare yourself for Jesus to merge with your body. Then, you invite Jesus to do so. Jesus lovingly accepts your invitation. He sits down where you sit. You feel his upper body merge with yours, then his legs. Feel the sensation of Jesus having merged with you as you have asked. His whole body is now merged with yours. Now, just sit in silence as you experience your connection with Jesus. Do not expect anything to happen as such. Just enjoy the experience of peace, love, calmness and connectedness.

*You can use a symbol other than Jesus who can represent the Holy Spirit if this works better for you.

While in either of these meditations, on occasion, the Holy Spirit may take the opportunity to pop a thought or an idea into your mind. If it does, be grateful for this added bonus.

Practicing one of these meditations for about five minutes every morning and every evening will greatly help foster a more conscious relationship with the Holy Spirit. However, this is not a ritualistic practice. So if you miss some of these meditation times there is no need to fret. It is not like someone is looking over your shoulder for an opportunity to punish you.

Your perspective on life is important. This meditation will help you gain a perspective on life that is more aligned with the thinking and perspective of the Holy Spirit. These newer perspectives of yours will automatically result in the chipping away at the web of misperceptions in your mind. One thing this will mean for you at a practical level is that where you before felt resistance towards something you wanted to do or achieve you may now find that this resistance is diminished or no longer there. Or you may find that something you wanted before you now no longer want. This is likely to indicate that whatever you wanted before would not have been helpful on your journey.

As you move through this process of improving your connection with the Holy Spirit, and with it increasingly choosing with the Holy Spirit, the ego *will* at times try to intercept your efforts. It wants to remain in charge of your life, remember. And it will often go to great lengths to achieve this, including very subtle ways that at first you may be oblivious to. In this context let me point out that the Holy Spirit always operates in the now moment; so all your communications from the Holy Spirit happen when your focus is in the present. This is why meditation is a very useful tool for connecting with the Holy Spirit. The ego cannot operate in the now moment. It relies on your memory of the past and your thoughts about the future. So the ego will encourage you to take your mind either back or forward in time. It is in these frames of mind that the ego is the reigning monarch, exerting its control over you. So if you find that one of your resistances have gone, the ego may try to take your mind to the memory of this resistance and try to convince you that this resistance is still there, and thereby try to re-introduce this resistance by re-introducing the ego story details into your mind. However, all you have to "do" is to overlook the ego voice and instead connect with the voice of the Holy Spirit. Equally, if one of your 'wants' has disappeared, the ego may try to either take your mind back or forward in time and through that try to convince you that you still want this because of this, that or the other. Again, when this happens just ignore it. Don't fight it with counter arguments. Just ignore it, and instead connect with the now moment and align yourself with the voice of the Holy Spirit.

I mentioned in the previous chapter that the Holy Spirit

sometimes makes you mindful of events in the past. Now I am saying that the Holy Spirit only operates in the now moment, in the present. This can seem inconsistent at first, so let me explain. The analogy that comes to mind is how all fairytales begin: "Once upon a time". When you listen to a fairytale, your mind does not go back to "once upon a time". Despite the reference being to the past, your mind remains in the present. Equally, when the Holy Spirit draws your attention to a misperception in the past, your mind remains in the present where you can hand the misperception over to the Holy Spirit for correction.

It can also at times be helpful to remind yourself that the Holy Spirit is always gentle, loving and caring towards you. So if this is your experience while you have, say, an intuition about something, it is likely that it is an intuition you can trust and, if applicable, you are advised to follow through on.

In seeking guidance through your experiences, whether you experience resistance or peace, either way you are very well placed for making progress. Having an understanding of the dynamics at play is an important ingredient as you work with these experiences. However, if you get caught up in the intellectual aspects of this practice at the expense of seeking and learning from your experiences, you will be prone to open the door for the ego. The ego is always keen to ask many questions. Some of which you may not be able to answer. If the ego finds you unable to answer one of its questions it will milk it much as it can. Like it tried to milk me about the question of how Jesus can have dictated *A Course in Miracles* if he is no longer in the Illusion. Luckily, through continuing to seek guidance through my experiences, I received an answer to that question after some time. If I had let the ego have its way, my progress along my path would have greatly slowed down. There may be times when there is no answer, or you find yourself unable to connect with the answer. At these times continue to seek experiences and be guided by them. This will ensure you chip away at your web of misperceptions until eventually you gain complete knowledge. Which brings us to the sixth Key: "you are in Reality". A place where there are no questions, only unchanging, certain and eternal knowledge.

Exercise

As an end of chapter exercise, we will now start to direct our focus even more towards the experiences we have while doing our exercises. After all, *it is about the experience, not the theory*. As well as doing one of the meditations introduced in this chapter, I would like you to re-do an exercise from a previous chapter of your choice; this time focusing primarily on the experiences you have when, as well as after, you do it. Do not think too much about the theory behind the exercise. Do not even think about whether you believe in the exercise or not. Just do it, and connect with the feelings and experiences; your *feelings* and *experiences* are your main guides toward experiencing who you are in truth, more so than theory and your thinking.

If you feel so guided, you can also choose an exercise from another previous chapter and again primarily focus on connecting with your feelings and experiences during and after the exercise.

Chapter 7

You are in Reality

So, the sixth Key is: **You are in Reality**. This has already been mentioned a few times in the previous Keys. Now, let's do a quick recap and look a bit deeper into what this entails.

The Illusion is purely a projection from your split mind. The vast majority of these projections are from the ego. These projections are ultimately rooted in your original guilt and fear. In turn, this generates emotional pain. But all the while you are not actually in the Illusion. *You are in Reality.* The Illusion is just a dream you are having while actually being in Reality[1]. Like in your nocturnal dreams, nothing within the dream is actually happening. It is all a figment of your mind's imagination. It is an optical illusion on a grand scale.

For some this can feel a bit depressing at first. It can seem like this thing we call life is a bit pointless. Equally though, it can be liberating. It can be liberating to know that nothing is really happening. And while our seeming experience is that it is happening, we can leave our thoughts and actions to the guidance of the Holy Spirit. We can hand the steering wheel over to the Holy Spirit.

Always remember that to experience autonomy away from Reality was your choice. Or rather, it was our collective choice. We collectively had this seeming idea of separation and autonomy from Reality, which then seemed to manifest in our mind. Over time, we made this seeming manifestation more and more complex, in an effort to hide from our denied perceived guilt and fear.

To me this adventure into separation is a bit like stepping into a labyrinth. It seems like a fun thing to do, so we go right ahead and step into it. Once we have done what we wanted to do in the labyrinth the challenge of getting back out is at first exciting. But after wandering around this labyrinth for a fair while the excitement of it slowly ebbs away. A while later it becomes a bit boring as we feel we have done all this before. It increasingly feels like we are going around in circles, making little or no progress.

I feel a bit like that about life sometimes. It feels like I have been there and done it all before. It is all becoming a bit old hat. Still, I cannot just step out of it unless I actually find my way out. The more I think of it as a bit old hat the longer it will stay that way, since it encourages thinking with the ego. However, luckily there is an alternative perspective; the perspective of the part of us that knows the layout of the labyrinth. We just need to connect with this part of ourselves and allow ourselves to be guided out of the labyrinth and back into our experience of Reality.

The labyrinth analogy also illustrates how real something can feel despite knowing that it is not your true reality. While in a labyrinth you know that it is just a way of entertaining yourself; it is an experience you chose to have, rather than it being your true everyday earthly experience. But if you have ever been in a labyrinth, you know that the need to find your way out feels very real while you are focused on this task. It becomes your very real experience of life during that time.

Equally, as far as your everyday life goes, you have now learned that it, and the world, are part of the Illusion. It isn't your true reality. Nevertheless, it feels very real to you while you are finding your way out of the world.

Some spiritual teachings suggest that you should befriend your ego. Well, the ego does not want to be your friend, certainly not in the true sense of the word. All it wants to do is to pretend to be your friend so that it can persuade you not to apply the type of tools presented in this book. Because it knows that if you do, it is the beginning of the end of its cherished game.

Let me introduce you to a simple yet powerful tool to marginalize the ego and speed up your progress out of this labyrinth we call life. I was first introduced to this tool in a Gary Renard workshop. I mentioned early on that the material presented in this book, if you apply it, will really get under the ego's skin. It was in a meditation that I felt that I should share this simple yet powerful tool with you. As I mentally made the decision to do so while still in meditation, I started to experience the same type of sensations as I felt when I first started my meditation practice. I started to experience a strange sensation in my mouth, tongue and upper chest area. My tongue felt swollen and took on an alien consistency. And the saliva in my mouth had a strange taste. My mouth began to go numb and my upper chest area experienced a slight contraction. Back then the ego was scared because it could sense that my newly found meditation practice was the beginning of it losing its grip on me. My decision to share this powerful tool in this book gave rise to the same fright in the ego. It does not want this tool widely shared. This time though, knowing that it represents the ego's fear, instead of instilling fear in me it sent me a strong signal that this tool is a powerful means towards undoing the ego. Here is the tool:

Every morning, give yourself a few seconds of silence during which you mentally ask the Holy Spirit to be in charge of your day.

How easy is that?! Yet it is very powerful. Casting our memory back to the analogy in Chapter 5 of you being the boss sitting in an office, this ensures that the door to your office stays open at all times.

Let us now go a bit deeper with this concept. The Holy Spirit will not force its communication on you. However, to invite a communication from the Holy Spirit is not always a conscious act. Often it is unconscious. This is why you also consciously connect with communication from the Holy Spirit even when you have not consciously invited it. However, when you put the

Holy Spirit in charge of your day you give it a wide open invitation to communicate with you whenever *it* feels it is appropriate. Furthermore, the Holy Spirit will communicate about whatever topic it feels is appropriate. If you find yourself in a situation where you have to act quickly and you do not have time to mentally connect with the Holy Spirit for inspiration, it will pre-empt you and pop the right thought into your mind for that situation. The overall effect is very powerful. The ego knows how powerful it is, and it appears to scare the hell out of it.

While you should not befriend the ego, nor should you view the ego as your enemy. Making the ego your enemy would acknowledge that the ego exists, which it doesn't. Rather, acknowledge your seeming experience of the ego's existence. At the same time, acknowledge to yourself that this is not who you are. In truth, only Reality exists and *you are in Reality*. So when you find yourself inclined to choose with the ego, this helps to get into the now moment and choose again. The ego is giving you experiences rooted in its twisted perception about, and paranoia towards, Reality, or God. Perceptions and paranoia rooted in unconscious denials. This is not you. *You are in Reality*. Acknowledging this understanding to yourself will gradually unhinge the ego; the ego's advances will get ever-less of your attention.

We concluded the last chapter by stating that by chipping away at your web of misperceptions you will eventually gain complete knowledge; complete knowledge of Reality. This chipping away results in the healing of what stands in the way of knowledge. And this chipping away is achieved by looking at the ego directly; without protecting nor fighting it. Just observe it together with the Holy Spirit and see it for what it is. Since what you are looking at and observing is the source of your fears, this might seem scary at first. But the more you persevere in looking at it together with the Holy Spirit and observing it together with the Holy Spirit the more you realize experientially that it is not real[2]. This leads to increased clarity and undoes confusion in equal measure, allowing you to move forward with more clarity and confidence. You will also experience the emergence of the realization that the ego's seeming effects can be dispelled merely by denying their existence[3].

We touched on the topic of being truly helpful in Chapter 2, including whether it is helpful to take action to help another. It was pointed out that this will depend on which lesson the Holy Spirit has in mind for this person. Putting the Holy Spirit in charge of your day will help you discern whether to take action or not. And as such, increase the likelihood of being truly helpful in your interactions with others.

With us all having unconscious guilt, there are people who are prone to feel that others are more worthy of their kindness. As such, they direct their kindness, in appropriate as well as inappropriate ways, toward others rather than toward themselves, feeling that others are more deserving of it. An attitude like this would not be aligned with the Holy Spirit. The Holy Spirit sees all as equally deserving, where truly helpful thoughts and actions are those that progress both you and your fellow human beings towards experiencing yourselves in truth, of experiencing yourselves in Reality.

On the topic of *you are in Reality*, let me share a mourning analogy with you. This may sound a bit morbid. But then again, how can a teaching that teaches that there is no death[4], but rather eternal life, be morbid? So here we go. When someone is about to pass away, what often holds him/her back is not feeling ready to die. Their lack of readiness is often linked to them feeling that someone needs them or they need someone. Or certain tasks in their life are unfinished. And all the people who had a mental attachment to this person or what this person stood for, or who otherwise associate this person with something unfinished, tend to have a mental attachment to this person. This mental attachment needs to be mourned. The mourning this results in for people may make it more difficult for the dying person to pass away. And once passed away it potentially makes the transition harder. But what if this person and all he/she stood for and represented were fully mourned before he/she passed away? To fully mourn them sets them free, in the same way as true love sets free. Imagine how easy it would be for this person to pass away and transition then.

Regaining your experience of being in Reality is like that. You need to mourn all mental attachments within the Illusion in order to get the ego story out of your mind. All these mental attachments need to be set free. Reality is unconditional love. And unconditional love sets free. Your mental attachments cannot vanish unless you set them free by lovingly mourning them, or mentally letting them go. And once they are fully mourned and free, you can see the love that they represent. Because, as Reality is all there is, so love is all there is. But this love can only be seen in what is set free, and to have attachments is to bind. So fully mourn your mental attachments, and set them, and with it yourself, free.

Remember, once a mental attachment is mourned you can still enjoy what you used to be mentally attached to. Now you can enjoy it with no mental or emotional charge attached to this enjoyment; the experience is free of expectations. You can now enjoy it with total freedom, which is a better experience, as well as an experience that allows more unconditional love to be put into the experience, and with it the scope to receive more love from the experience.

Some of your mental attachments you may however feel a stronger allegiance to. But remember, in truth you are not a body, since there is no form. In truth, you do not have individuality, since there is no separation. And you are not actually going anywhere since you are already in Reality. *You are in Reality* now, have always been there and will always be there. The reason why you have an experience of being in the Illusion is because you have bought into the ego story, and through the ego story you have made mental attachments. Remember, this is all happening in your mind. Whatever you see out there is just a projection from your mind. Without mental attachments to the ego story, there would be no ego projection. There would be nothing for the ego to project. And you would eventually not even have an experience of being in the Illusion. Therefore, in order to regain your experience of Reality it is mandatory to first fully mourn, or mentally let go of, your mental attachments to what the Illusion seems to contain. I use the phrase "seems to" here, since in truth the Illusion contains nothing; you mourn nothing. The mental attachments you mourn are only imaginary, similar to you gaining attachment to a person in a fictional movie you are watching. So be a happy mourner and lovingly mentally divest yourself from the movie screen of the world, the ego story and the resultant seeming Illusion. The result will be an experience of true love, of total freedom.

This gets me to think of Tony Blair's premiership in the United Kingdom. I lived in England during his time as prime minister. There was a time when the press in England used to call him Teflon Tony; no issues seemed to stick to him. They were always somehow deflected like water is deflected by Teflon. Once everything in the Illusion is mourned you will become like Teflon. Nothing will affect your peace of mind and happiness because you are fully aligned with the Holy Spirit; you do not have a mental attachment to anything. This does not mean that you do not take action, show affection or compassion and in general behave in a way that is kind to another. The Holy Spirit wants you to be truly helpful to others on their path. It probably also wants you to be normal in your interactions with others. Always aim to be kind and loving. Jesus reached the stage of Teflon Jesus. He still did all that he did. And most would agree that what he did was good. Being truly Teflon means you are no longer influenced by the ego; the Illusion Circle is deflated and now contains the Holy Spirit only. The ego only has a hold on you for as long as you have mental attachments to the ego story. Without such mental attachments, all you think and do, while still having a body and a conscious awareness of the Illusion, are as willed by the Holy Spirit. You are now choosing with, and coming from, the Holy Spirit all the time, never from the ego.

However, you should not try to become a Teflon person by ignoring everything you feel like ignoring. But nor should you be like Velcro and let everything you feel a resistance to get stuck on you. In the spirit of Tony Blair inspirations, who also used the catch phrase 'the third way' during his premiership, in this instance there is indeed a third way. This leads us to the seventh and last Key: "remember Reality and experience yourself".

Exercise

In order to help you connect more with the Holy Spirit, do the recommended short exercise of putting the Holy Spirit in charge every morning you have a chance to do so. In the beginning, it may be more effective to close your eyes and quiet your mind as you do it. However, this is not strictly necessary.

Chapter 8

Remember Reality and Experience Yourself

So, the seventh Key is: **Remember Reality and experience yourself.**

So what is this third way? Well, we are now at the seventh and last Key. This is where the rubber really hits the road. The tools we have learned so far to chip away at the web of misperceptions in our mind are powerful. However, we are now ready to add the turbo charger.

The tool we are about to learn is at the core of what this teaching is about. You are now at the home stretch of this book. If you apply the tool presented in this chapter, you may also be on the home stretch of your cycle of life and death. You may soon naturally leave dualistic spiritual teachings behind and truly practice non-dualistic spirituality. All dualistic spirituality hurdles can be left behind you, leaving the coast clear to progress to the end of the cycle of life and death.

What we have learned thus far has been in preparation for this tool. If you apply this tool, the rest takes care of itself. This tool will help speed up your journey to your ultimate goal, to know yourself and experience yourself as being in Reality. To achieve this, as this Key points out, you must first remember Reality. And by now you are very clear on what part of our mind remembers Reality; namely, the Holy Spirit. The Holy Spirit needs your co-operation to fully refresh your memory. Since you are the boss, the one who chooses between the ego's and the Holy Spirit's voices, the Holy Spirit needs you to choose its voice so that it can assist you in chipping away at the misperceptions in your mind. As you make this choice, there is a perfect tool for assisting you in your alignment with the Holy Spirit's voice. This tool is the third way. In *A Course in Miracles*, this tool is called *forgiveness*. If you have had a resistance to biblical words this resistance may by now have diminished or gone away. In any case, like the meaning of the word Holy Spirit in *A Course in Miracles* being different to its biblical counterpart, so is the meaning of the word forgiveness different.

So what *is* forgiveness? The first thing that tends to come into people's minds in connection with forgiveness is sin; there is some sort of sin to be forgiven. Therefore, in order to understand the true meaning of forgiveness it is important to understand that there is no sin[1]. How can there be sin? There is only Reality. There is no sin in Reality. The concept of sin is just another construct of the ego; another one of ego's tools to keep us stuck in the Illusion.

Another dominant thought in connection with traditional forgiveness is that it is something external to us that does the forgiveness, like God. But God does not forgive because God never condemns[2]. There is no condemnation in Reality. Here you will learn that it is always you, together with the Holy Spirit, who performs the forgiveness. Condemnation is of the ego, and when you choose with the ego you condemn alongside it. By choosing forgiveness with the Holy Spirit, you can undo your ego aligned condemnations, and experience peace instead. It is through forgiveness that peace is attained[3].

As a general statement, the key to forgiveness is to understand that thoughts of the ego are meaningless, as is the world of the Illusion[4]. How can something that doesn't exist have meaning? The fact that it can't makes this statement vitally important. Therefore, I will state it again: '*the key to forgiveness is to understand that thoughts of the ego are meaningless, as is the world of the Illusion*'.

We have already mentioned the ego thought of sin. Another typical thought of the ego is that it is important to do certain things. In the same vein, it is also important not to do certain other things. This thought and behavioral trait is often also found in spiritual teachings; e.g., some spiritual teachings focus on celibacy. The reason for celibacy is presented as the need to relinquish the mental attachment to the lust of the body. However, as far as mental attachments go, being focused on *not* doing or having something is just as much a mental attachment as being focused on doing or having something.

In the context of mental attachments to be mourned, as mentioned in the previous chapter, the focus is on letting them go, or releasing them. The focus is *not* on not having them. This is a subtle, yet important, distinction between these two focuses.

Forgiveness happens in conjunction with the Holy Spirit. As such, it is non-judgmental. In fact, it is diametrically opposed to judgment; you cannot forgive and judge at the same time. You either judge or you forgive. In the context of doing or not doing something, such a decision is based on judgment. To forgive would be to acknowledge your understand that attachment to such a decision is based on thoughts of the ego and are therefore meaningless.

The celibacy issue also brings up the issue of putting the cart before the horse. While this can be useful at times, it should be used with care. We are probably all aware of the issues that have surfaced in the Catholic Church as a result of celibacy. Typically, the safest and most effective approach is to be honest with yourself and true to yourself. It is through being honest with yourself that you become aware of your resistance experiences. And it is by being true to yourself that you choose to release these resistances to the Holy Spirit, and chip away at your web of misperceptions; thereby chip away these resistances. And whatever resistance you experience, it is okay. There is no judgment involved in this process. It is all about releasing, or letting go of, misperceptions, or the ego story, for the related correction of the mind to be done by the Holy Spirit.

In the context of what a spiritual person should or should not do, there are teachings and literature that prescribe behavior rather than empower people to follow the guidance of the Holy

Spirit. *Your* relationship with the Holy Spirit is unique to you. It is not like anybody else's. For example, there are spiritual people who are vegeterians and there are spiritual people who hunt animals. There are spiritual people who do not drink alcohol and there are spiritual people who enjoy alcohol. It is not for any one of us to say what is right or wrong. We do not know what guidance they receive from the Holy Spirit, or how their most graceful and effective path home looks like. Bottom line, there are no 'should have done' or 'shouldn't have done'. If you have been haunted by those, rescue is at hand. Again you will see that anything to do with what you should or should not do is rooted in judgment. You may argue that you cannot operate in the world without making judgments along the way. And this would be true. However, by practicing forgiveness you would be practicing non-judgment. This practice of non-judgment will eventually get you into a space where there is an ever-diminishing need for judgment. And eventually, you will no longer need to judge. Because, remember, the part of your mind that judges, and thereby keeps you in the labyrinth of the Illusion, is the ego. If you want to find the exit out of the labyrinth of the Illusion, it is your forgiveness practice, and your resulting perceptions and Holy Spirit guided actions, which will guide you to that exit; perceptions and guided actions rooted in love that transcend the need to judge. Remember, all aspects of Reality are really all one and the same. So love is knowledge. Love always knows what to do.

As mentioned in the previous chapter, to think of life as old hat and the world you live in as one you are unable to connect with is not a helpful attitude. And your attitude is important. It is a lot more helpful to be of the attitude that the forgiveness opportunities that will get you out of this labyrinth will always come your way. And be intent on making use of your opportunities to forgive.

So, let's now look at the practical details of how to forgive. The process of forgiveness, as with everything else that this teaching is about is a mental process. Let's break it into four steps:

1. When you feel that your peace of mind is disturbed by judgment, whether of a situation and/or a person, stop that thought and mentally connect with the Holy Spirit* and acknowledge this judgment;
2. Then remind yourself that your ego mind made all this up and that there is actually nothing out there;
3. Remind yourself that you are not your ego thoughts, but rather, you are safely at home in Reality^; and
4. Then completely forgive the judgment of the situation and/or person and release it to the Holy Spirit* and trust that the Holy Spirit* will chip away the related part of your web of misperceptions.

*If a symbol other than the Holy Spirit works better for you please use this instead.
^ If a symbol other than Reality works better for you, e.g. God or Source, please use this instead.

The forgiveness process is always done with love, since it is always done with the Holy Spirit, which is forever loving. It also leaves you with the experience of what ACIM refers to as a Holy Instant.

After you have forgiven an event, have no expectation about how the related healing of the mind will manifest. Simply trust the Holy Spirit. It does not matter whether you can see the results or not. Just know that if you do the forgiveness with the Holy Spirit it will have an impact[5].

With forgiveness, a positive circle of an ever-improved alignment with the Holy Spirit and an ever-diminishing web of misperceptions unfolds. Again, as with most concepts in this teaching, the forgiveness process is simple. But that does not mean that it is easy to implement. After all, you have been under the control of the ego for quite some time. In effect, this teaching is saying that the only true judgment is the verdict of being sinless and guiltless, a verdict of innocence. This is completely at odds with anything in the story the ego has fed you. Implementing this new perspective will need some practice and mental discipline.

If you find yourself resisting following the guidance of the Holy Spirit, this is a judgment against the Holy Spirit, and can be forgiven through this forgiveness process accordingly.

In terms of where you are at now, you are attracted to guilt and fear. And so am I. That is just the nature of the pull of the unconscious mind, the pull of our denials. Without unconscious guilt and fear I would not be a student of ACIM, you would not be reading this book, and there would be no universe of bodies and things. At some level, you think you deserve to be guilty and fearful, and you have become addicted to it. The good news though is that you are now in the process of acknowledging your addiction to guilt and fear, and as such becoming ready to start to look it squarely in the eye, with the Holy Spirit. This addiction, and your mind's attraction to the ego story, is healed through forgiveness.

This might sound like a lot of work. But keep in mind, this work needs to be done some time. You can delay it to a later time, but it is not as though you can bypass it. The web of misperceptions in your mind will not go away by itself. Death does not take it away. It just delays it to the next or an even later lifetime. You hear all this talk about babies having pure minds, which then are corrupted by the world. Well, they come in with a web of misperceptions accumulated in previous lives. Your mind is the *only* thing you take with you into your grave, so to speak. So you may as well spend time in this lifetime on something that will actually benefit you beyond this lifetime. Anyway, life is in many ways hard work. My experience is that, while it takes a bit of mental discipline to apply these concepts, my life as a whole flows with greater ease now than it did before. And I am more at peace. So we might as well get on with forgiveness now, right? As the saying goes, there is no time like the present.

To help us develop the mental discipline to forgive, let me re-introduce the Teflon and Velcro aspects of your mind. We have moments where things just wash over us, as if they hit Teflon; in these moments we are pretty carefree. There are also moments when certain things get stuck in our mind, as if it has hit a Velcro surface. And the thoughts they give rise to will not leave us alone. It can be something that has just happened, something that our mind takes us back to that is bothering us, or some concern we have about the future. What is characteristic of all of them is that they have taken our mind out of the present moment, to either the immediate or distant past or future. It has taken our mind into the domain of the ego. Through the forgiveness process, we can bring ourselves back to the present moment. You start by stopping the ego thought, and instead connect with the Holy Spirit and acknowledge the Velcro thought and feeling that you had (which always contains an element of judgment). You then remind yourself that this Velcro thought and feeling is made up by the ego and does not actually exist. You then remind yourself that you are not that ego thought, but rather, you are residing in Reality; and then completely forgive it and release the ego thought to the Holy Spirit and trust that healing of the mind will take place.

Let's go through an example. You find yourself worrying about money. In your judgment, your money situation is worrying. So first, stop the money worry and instead connect with the Holy Spirit. And while connected, acknowledge your worry about money. Secondly, remind yourself that this money worry is all made up and does not actually exist. Thirdly, remind yourself that the money worry is not you. Rather, you are safely at home in Reality. Fourthly, completely forgive the money worrying thought and release it, in trust, to the Holy Spirit.

When you have completed this forgiveness process, the Holy Spirit will chip away at the related misperceptions in your mind. Continue to stay in the present moment and relax. Feel the love and warmth that accompany the ego misperception chipping work now being done by the Holy Spirit. Mentally acknowledge this experience. Experiences like these are what we seek as stepping-stones along our path; they nurture us in preparation for the next step on our journey.

These Velcro, or lack of peace of mind, experiences are a good place to start since they involve emotional pain. To the extent we have a mantra, it is: "I can choose peace of mind instead of this."[6]. Forgiveness is your tool for experiencing peace of mind; forgiveness is the protein for the peace-of-mind-muscle.

Pain tends to get our attention. You can use pain as your reminder to choose peace of mind instead, to choose to go through the forgiveness process. The forgiveness process, applied to whatever is causing you emotional pain, brings you into the present moment. And the experience you are left with, as you continue to stay in the present moment for some time after you have completed the forgiveness process, will be very different to the experience you had before you forgave. Typically, you will feel peace of mind. This experience nurtures you and encourages you to continue your journey.

Keeping things simple is helpful as you embark on your journey of forgiveness. So let us call a spade a spade; emotional pain is always of the ego. There is no need to use the spade, i.e. the pain, to dig into the sub-conscious. Leave this digging to the Holy Spirit. Knowing and acknowledging that the emotional pain is of the ego is enough to satisfy the stated need to look the ego squarely in the eye. All you need to do next is to forgive, together with the Holy Spirit, the thought that gave rise to this pain. It is that simple. Sure, it is not always easy and it takes a bit of willingness and practice. But it is that simple.

If you have a moment you want to dedicate to forgiveness then do so. You do not have to wait for a Velcro moment if one is not already present. Instead, you can for example bring your mind to what tends to push your buttons. We are all prone to have our buttons pushed at times. Well, these buttons are resistances in our mind. With no resistance, or mental attachment, in our ego mind there would be no buttons to push. And by the way, the Holy Spirit is not into time, since time does not exist in Reality. To bring your mind to something in the past and performing the forgiveness process on it works perfectly well. So you can cast your mind back in time and remind yourself of what pushes your buttons. Then perform the forgiveness process on that. Equally, if you find that your mind makes you think about something in the past that upsets you, then that is an indication that now is a good time to do the forgiveness process on this. You may also experience a concern about the future. Again, this concern is another emotional pain symbolic of something unconsciously denied in your mind. This presents an opportunity to forgive this concern about the future by reminding yourself, together with the Holy Spirit, that you are not what has given rise to this concern. Rather, you are safely at home in Reality. Then completely forgive this concern and release it to the Holy Spirit.

You may have heard spiritual teachings tell you that you bring your experiences upon yourself. And you need to own them and take responsibility for them. While this is true since, everything out there is a projection from your mind, it is however not necessary to dwell on them and try to understand how this can be. Remember the spade analogy; painful and uncomfortable experiences are always of the ego part of the split mind. The vast majority of what you project onto your screen of the world is unconscious, so to try to get your conscious mind around it all is going to become a distraction and move you along your path at a snail's pace. The Holy Spirit has got its head around all this already so you don't have to. You might as well delegate it accordingly. If the Holy Spirit deems it helpful for you to know the underlying reason for the emotional pain it will let you know. All you need to do is to own up to the experience of emotional pain and perform the forgiveness process on the experienced emotional pain.

Often what upsets you today, or what has upset you in the past, involves another person. It may be a person you are angry with or feel some other upset towards. Since ultimately the emotion or feeling that arises in your mind is symbolic of something unconsciously denied in *your* mind, the presented forgiveness process still works. A part of your mind has brought this person and situation into manifestation in order to facilitate a certain projection. You have made a forgiveness opportunity for yourself within which another person is also involved. ACIM states that one of its most important lessons is that you are never upset with another because of anything to do with them, but only with things that have to do with you. And that learning this lesson will greatly speed up your progress towards happiness[7].

Another perspective that can be useful to remember is that we are all in Reality, having a seeming experience of being in the Illusion; this other person is also in Reality going through a seeming experience of being in the Illusion. Feeling as lost as you, if not more lost; being love in truth, but not being able to express it or give it fully while having this seeming experience of the Illusion. Just consciously seeing it from this perspective is perception changing in its own right.

In order to acknowledge your oneness in Reality with this person, who has seemingly, but not really, brought to the fore of your conscious mind these Velcro emotions and feelings, you can change your forgiveness process to:

1. When you have been upset by another, stop that thought and mentally connect with the Holy Spirit* and

acknowledge the thought;

2. Then remind yourself that this upset, which was a judgment, is made up by the ego and that there is actually nothing out there;

3. Remind yourself that neither you nor this other person is as perceived by your ego thoughts, but rather, you are both safely at home in Reality^; and

4. Then completely forgive the person and the upset, and release it to the Holy Spirit* and trust that the Holy Spirit* will chip away the related part of your web of misperceptions.

*If a symbol other than the Holy Spirit works better for you please use this instead.

^If a symbol other than Reality works better for you, e.g. God or Source, please use this instead.

Again, let's look at an example. Someone said something that you found hurtful. They may or may not have intended to be hurtful, but you took offence to what they said. You judge them as unfair, and you cannot get the episode fully out of your mind. In this situation, firstly, connect with the Holy Spirit. While connected in this way, mentally acknowledge that you're upset. Secondly, remind yourself that the reason for this upset is rooted in the ego and that this reason does not actually exist. Thirdly, remind yourself that neither you nor this person are those ego generated upsetting thoughts. In truth, you are both in Reality. Fourthly, completely forgive the person and the upset, and release it to the Holy Spirit and trust that the related healing of your mind is taking place.

Since minds are joined, a healing will also take place in the other person's mind when forgiveness takes place. As well as experiencing a change in yourself after applying the forgiveness process you may also perceive a change in the other person, since your projection is no longer there for that person to mirror back to you. So ultimately you are the greatest beneficiary of your forgiveness.

Recently someone told me one of his powerful forgiveness stories. This story shows that forgiveness can have immediate effects, both on you and the ones the forgiveness exercise includes. He, let's call him Michael, was having romantic relationship issues. He was a young guy, and had two romantic relationships behind him; both of which had ended badly. So Michael had decided not to enter into any more romantic relationships. Then one day he came upon an opportunity to attend a weekend *A Course in Miracles* workshop that was going to focus on the healing of romantic relationships. It was over two days and Michael decided to sign up for it. During the first day of the workshop they did a very powerful forgiveness exercise to heal past and, for whom it was applicable, current romantic relationships. In the evening, following the first day of the workshop, both of Michael's ex romantic partners called him, and they spoke in very reconciliatory terms. Michael could not believe the effect of the forgiveness exercise he had done during the workshop and was excited about sharing it with the other workshop participants the following day. When he did, they were amazed. Not because of what had happened to him, but because exactly the same had happened to them too; to each and every one of them. They all had been contacted by ex-partners.

I found that story so amazing; this is what is possible. This illustrates how powerful *your* forgiveness can be. I am not suggesting that you can expect results like this every time you forgive. But it does demonstrate that it is very possible. After all, it did not only happen to just one person, it happened to all of them.

In Michael's case, the story did not end there; someone had been making advances to Michael. However, Michael had not been receptive to them. After the workshop he was receptive, and within a week of the workshop Michael was in a new relationship; one that turned out to be wonderful.

This is a good time to do a forgiveness exercise on your own. Do it on the first thing that comes to mind. Whether it involves a person or not doesn't matter. All that matters is that whatever it relates to has a Velcro sense, or lack of peace of mind or emotional pain, associated with it ... Okay, this event has now come into your mind. But before you do the forgiveness process on it, notice the level of density you feel about your state of mind. Then grade the level of density on a scale from 1 to 10, with one being bliss and ten being hatred ... Now that you have determined the level, perform the forgiveness process in your mind as described above. Yes, do that now, with your eyes closed, before you read on.

Now that you have done your forgiveness, notice the current level of density in your mind. Is it lighter? On a scale from 1 to 10, with one being bliss and ten being hatred, what level would you say it is now?

A note of caution at this point: the ego is not going to let you embark on your journey of forgiveness without a fight. For example, it may tell you that the emotional pain is worth investigating further. And the person inflicting it on you is guilty as charged. This is after all largely what defines the ego story; projection of denied guilt so that we can see another as guilty, rather than seeing it from the Holy Spirit's perspective and release the guilt buried in the canyons of our unconscious mind. Our tendency, as creatures of habit, is to align our perceived individuality with a view of us being the victim of guilty perpetrators. The ego will take every opportunity to remind you of this; of you being a victim. But you now know that this is not what or who you are. This story of being victimized by guilty perpetrators is not a story to be treasured. Instead use the emotional pain this story gives rise to as an opportunity for forgiveness, and as such release this emotional pain from your mind.

You are also likely to experience occasions where even though you have forgiven a person and/or a situation, the emotional pain that made you perform the forgiveness comes back. Whenever you think about it, you still do not have a sense of Teflon, but rather of the sticky Velcro. It is my experience that in a number of instances I need to forgive the same thing more than once. There will have been some chipping away at my web of misperceptions as a result of the forgiveness I have done, but some of the misperceptions that gave rise to the Velcro feeling or emotion in the first place are still there. And this is not surprising. It is a bit like the often used analogy of peeling an onion. Often there are a few layers in the web of misperceptions that need to be chipped away before all aspects of the misperceptions that gave rise to the Velcro feeling or emotional pain are chipped away. Remember, the web of misperceptions was not built in a day.

A work example is often good to demonstrate this. You turn up at work, and you forgive the events and the people who you wish worked somewhere else. Then you turn up for work the next day and the same people are still there, and similar events take place. I have not worked in the traditional sense of the word for the last few years so I do not have any personal hot off the press examples. However, an *A Course in Miracles* student I know does. For the purpose of this example, let us call this person John. John works in a workplace and a work environment with a great variety of people, including people from a diverse cultural background. And the workplace attracts a few ego types. You know, the 'look how wonderful I am at my work' types. And 'don't come here and tell me what to do/how to do it' types. And if a mistake has been done it is never their fault, or it is simply brushed under the carpet. And with the cultural diversity there are sometimes communication issues and/or, shall we call it, etiquette issues, e.g. women can't talk to men as freely as men can talk to women. The work is project based, so when a new project team is assembled, and the project commences, there are usually a number of forgiveness opportunities that present themselves. Things are forgiven, and still issues persist. And the people continue to stay on the project. But what John finds is that through diligent forgiveness work a number of the people change their behaviors and attitudes. And with it a number of the issues dissolve and disappear. So John finds that forgiveness works. And John senses that these forgiveness opportunities all serve a purpose; and that the current work environment is the best environment for the forgiveness he needs to do at this time. Let us also be reminded that while the actual events may not change a great deal as a result of forgiveness, your perception of these events will[8]. You will be a lot more at peace with them. They will not push your buttons in the way they used to. You will have more of a Teflon feeling. As a result you will handle situations that arise better too.

Another thing John senses is that there are certain people in that work place who he is meant to meet. Often John is meant to have an impact on these people, and often it is the other way around. Remember, there is only one mind. Minds are joined. And, at an unconscious level, you understand that people are here to help each other on their respective journeys. It's like life is some sort of dance of learning and unlearning opportunities. The specific reason why certain things are taking place or a certain person crosses your path is in itself not important. What is important is to tune into the communication from the Holy Spirit and to trust and follow the coaxing you receive, whatever situation you find yourself in, and whether it involves another person or not. Through your forgiveness work, you will gain the experiences and the greater clarity of communication with the Holy Spirit that enables you to do just that.

Wherever you are on your journey, it is important to accept and take ownership of where you are. Again, be true to yourself. And choose to move forward from wherever you are. Do not choose to move forward from wherever you would have liked to be. You may feel there are certain situations in which you should not become angry. But if your experience is that those situations make you angry, you are well advised to own up to this and perform the forgiveness work that will get you to a space where those situations no longer make you angry. Don't continue the denial of it. This will just add to the web of misperceptions in your mind. Be honest with yourself as you do this work. This is very important, so I will state it again. Be honest with yourself as you do this work.

Equally important, do not beat yourself up if you are not as far along as you would like to be, or as maybe you thought you were. Only the ego wants to beat you up. Instead, be grateful for your newfound awareness. This new awareness is going to serve you better. Being honest with yourself wins the day; it wins you the best forgiveness opportunities.

Along similar lines, whenever you choose to forgive something, check in with yourself how sincere you are about forgiving it. Do you just *want* to forgive it or are you *willing* to embrace the forgiveness of it? As we touched upon earlier, including in the Freud healing example, there will be differing degrees of unconscious resistance lurking beneath the surface of your conscious mind. Some forgiveness issues will have stronger resistances attached to them than others. So after you have forgiven something, if the emotional pain associated with it persists, there is likely to be a subconscious part of your mind that is resisting the dismantling of that part of the web of misperceptions so that only a very small part of the web of misperceptions is chipped away. And the portion that is chipped away may be too small for you to feel that the forgiveness made any difference. If this happens, do not get upset about it. This happens from time to time. Just acknowledge it. Next time you team up with the Holy Spirit to forgive it, acknowledge that you are experiencing a resistance to this forgiveness opportunity. And acknowledge that neither what you are forgiving nor the resistance to what you are forgiving is you. If you are sincere about working through it, this sharper focus on the forgiveness opportunity at hand is likely to help convert your wanting to forgive it into willingness to forgive it. Again, you are the boss. The level of sincerity with which you choose to approach each forgiveness opportunity is *your* choice. As Michael's story demonstrates, with willingness changes can take place in your mind as well as in the minds of others, and in the physical world. After all, minds are joined, as per the collapsed cone/pyramid analogy in Chapter 2. And the world you perceive, see and experience is a mirror of the mind's inner condition. The mind is always the cause. Only a change in the cause can alter the effect; can make changes on the screen of the world.

The process of forgiveness is indeed practical. An example, which further demonstrates this well, is the experience of holding anger and grievance towards another. You may spend years holding onto this anger and grievance; draining yourself of energy and happiness. By forgiving them in the space of minutes, or at worst a handful of forgiveness processes of a few minutes each, the time and mind effort you have dispensed on your anger and grievance will no longer be part of your experience going forward; you can instead experience more peace and happiness right now.

When you forgive it is your attitude that is most important. It is important to have an attitude that is aligned with the forgiveness process I have provided in this Key. Such an attitude is also consistent with and draws on the six prior Keys. The word for word mental articulation of the forgiveness process given in this chapter is less important. With practice, you will probably find that the mental forgiveness process speeds up. Certain mental articulations become irrelevant because they will then be so ingrained in your view of the world that it becomes redundant to specifically mentally remind yourself of them. Gary Renard's

The Disappearance of the Universe promises you that "Once you really understand [the forgiveness attitude] then it will become a permanent part of you. If these kinds of thoughts become dominant in your mind, then it can't help but mean the Holy Spirit is taking over"[9].

You can trust that the right forgiveness opportunities will present themselves. There is no need to chase or look for forgiveness opportunities. Since *it is all in the mind*, the mind will be your guide. Your right mind, where the Holy Spirit resides, will be your guide. Just be alert to your forgiveness opportunities and acquire the mental discipline to do the forgiveness work when they arise. Becoming mindful of your Velcro feelings is a good place to start.

You are likely to experience times when you do not feel like forgiving one of those Velcro feelings. Maybe you have had a bust up with someone and the last thing you feel like doing right now is to forgive him/her. That is okay. It happens to most of us at times. In these situations, instead forgive your resistance to forgive. Mentally connect with the Holy Spirit and acknowledge that you do not want to forgive this person right now. Then remind yourself that it is because of your ego that you do not want to forgive this person right now. Acknowledge that this lack of willingness to forgive this person is symbolic of something unconsciously denied in your mind. Then, as before, remind yourself that you are not that, rather you are safely at home in Reality. You may also want to acknowledge that this person you had a bust up with is not that and is also safely at home in Reality. And with that completely forgive the resistance to forgive this person and release it to the Holy Spirit.

Also, it may be useful to remember what the Illusion is. It is nothing. This means that nothing actually happens in the Illusion. This bust up, or anything else for that matter, did not actually happen[10]. I often find this a useful reminder when I find it difficult to bring myself to forgive something or someone.

And, as Gary Renard's book *The Disappearance of the Universe* counsels us; "It might help you to remember that *you're* the one whom forgiveness helps. You don't always have to care personally about the person you're forgiving. Your job is simply to correct your misperceptions, and it isn't against the rules to know that you can't help but benefit because of it."[11] Forgiving someone is the ultimate example of giving is receiving. So be generous with your forgiveness.

In truth, there is nothing to forgive. But our daily experience is not one of truth. It is one of the Illusion. For as long as this is the case, forgiveness is the most potent tool towards acquiring the experience of truth, of Reality.

Along those lines, let's touch upon something often referred to as level confusion. The levels it refers to are the level of oneness versus the level of separation, the latter being the level of your day-to-day experiences. At the level of oneness, or at the level of higher truths if you will, you may use phrases like 'it's all the same', 'there is only one ego', 'it's all an illusion'. And you may use these higher truths as something to hide behind; 'it is all an illusion so why should I care anyway?' and 'it's all the same anyway, so why should I care?'. In the same way as the Holy Spirit uses your seeming experiences in the world made by the ego to present forgiveness opportunities, the ego may use these oneness statements presented by the Holy Spirit as a means to try to keep you stuck in the ego's story. This is an example of where the fifth Key is important to remember: *it is all about the experience, not the theory*. The ego may on occasion try to take your attention to the oneness theory and the ego's interpretation of the oneness theory as a means of discouraging you from using your day-to-day experiences as a means to become aware of forgiveness opportunities. Do not be persuaded by the ego to fall into these thought patterns. After all, it is your day-to-day experiences that present you with your forgiveness opportunities. We are reminded in *The Disappearance of the Universe* that;

"It is at the level of your experience that your training must take place"[12]. So to re-iterate, do not fall into the trap of level confusion, confusing the importance of the oneness theory as being more important than using your day-to-day experiences as forgiveness opportunities. An understanding of the oneness and equality of all things is helpful and important, but such an understanding on its own will not get you far. It is *true forgiveness*, which this understanding allows, that propels you forward on your journey home. Therefore, of the two choices referred to in the fourth Key, make sure you choose forgiveness with the Holy Spirit over attaching undue importance to metaphysical truths.

In bringing this chapter to an end, for the avoidance of any possible confusion, please be reminded that whether your emotional reactions are of the Teflon or Velcro type, eventually you will have to forgive them all. Even the Teflon ones need examining. As mentioned earlier, all your perceptions will eventually have to be re-looked at with the Holy Spirit. But let us not get ahead of ourselves here. Starting with the Velcro ones will most probably suffice in order to get some good momentum into this practice for you. And once you have gained momentum you can always check in with the Holy Spirit and see whether it is time to cast your net wider; but, having said that, you should watch out for the Teflon feelings that nurture your ego. For example, say that your job involves having people working for you. And you have gotten your subordinates to display exactly the type of behaviors and work ethic you would like them to display. Which may include getting you a coffee every morning and saying 'yes, boss' to all your suggestions. As long as they do this, you may have a Teflon experience. However, it is your web of misperceptions that have made you instill these behaviors among your subordinates.

Exercise

It is time to start forgiving, for you to do true forgiveness whenever you feel loss of peace of mind. I do not expect you to be able to do this every time you feel a loss of peace of mind, but do it as often as you find possible. However, we have covered a lot of ground thus far, so to help you along with this let's next go through some reminders.

Chapter 9

Some Reminders

Reality is everything. Attributes we can ascribe to Reality for the benefit of making it a less abstract concept are:

- Permanent;
- Unchanging;
- Eternal;
- Spirit (i.e. no form)
- Whole;
- Love (Unconditional);
- Peace;
- One;
- Knowing; and
- Creation.

This is who you are. This is your home. This is where you are.

The Illusion is not[1]. Through the ego you have managed to convince yourself that you are in the Illusion. As a result, your seeming experience is one of being in the Illusion. The conscious part of your mind has the experience of being in the Illusion.

You have the experience of being in the Illusion because of mental attachments, mental attachments to all the little fish of the ego story. And what are the little fish of the ego, the little fish of the world, other than something that is destined to wither and die. Like the fish in the watering hole that withered and died, completely at the mercy of the system of the ego. Everything made in the Illusion is destined to wither and die. It is a system where everything is impermanent and must therefore eventually wither and die. This is what you have become attached to. And in the process you have forgotten about the big fish, Reality, eternal life, yourself as who you are in truth.

It is all in the mind, and therefore the mind causes your experiences. You can change the effects, or your experiences in the world, by changing your mind. To make changes happen is made easier by the fact that **there is no form, only content**. It is not as though you have to make changes to anything physical. Nor do you have to change others. It all starts and ends with yourself; your mind. All you have to focus on, together with the part of your split mind that is the Holy Spirit, is yourself and your mental attachments. It is your mental attachments, rooted in denied unconscious guilt and fear, which fills the world through your projections. These mental attachments make themselves known to you in part through emotional pain. And **there are no coincidences** as the tapestry of life allows events to unfold. These events make the backdrops and the cues that become the catalysts that guide you. You will always be in an opportune place and be presented with opportune events for forgiveness. The tapestry of life is rich enough for the perfect forgiveness opportunities to arise when you are ready to work through them. And **there are always only two choices**. By choosing one you give up the other[2]. You are the boss, so when these forgiveness opportunities arise it is you who decide whether you take them on, or whether you would rather listen to the ego's excuse for not taking them on. You can either choose with the ego, and stay stuck within the labyrinth of the Illusion, or you can choose with the Holy Spirit, and start making your way towards its exit. As you choose the latter, be guided and encouraged by the experiences that come your way. **It is about the experience, not the theory**. While it is important to understand the ego and its ways as you unhinge it via forgiveness, dwelling too much on the theory around it is likely to divert your attention away from catching your forgiveness opportunities. Your experiences resulting from your forgiveness work will eventually show you that **you are in Reality** and subsequently lead you to fully **remember Reality and experience yourself**.

There will be times when projection will give you relief from emotional pain. But be careful not to be encouraged by this. As with everything else within the ego story, such a fix will only be a temporary one. A projection is just a recycling mechanism and eventually it will catch up with you again. Forgiveness puts the cause of the emotional pain in the trash, never to be the cause of this experienced again.

To experientially know who you are is your end goal. This goal implies that you will no longer experience any guilt or fear in your mind. The entire web of misperceptions has been chipped away; there are no longer any hooks by which the ego can get your attention. Your attention is entirely with the Holy Spirit. You have uncovered your true self. You are naked, stripped of all the ego seductions. You are free. You are free to leave the Illusion behind and experience Reality only. Once you release the Illusion and allow yourself to be totally embraced by Reality, you will be aware of Reality only; the Illusion will not even be a distant memory[3]. You have awoken from the seeming dream. There is nothing to remember from this seeming dream since the Illusion isn't, nor has it ever been.

The Holy Spirit is your teacher[4], guiding you to your experience of Reality.

At this point I would also like to mention something that Jesus told his disciple Thomas, referenced in the Gospel of Thomas. Jesus told Thomas that if he were to know the beginning he would also know the end[5]. To experience what Jesus was talking about is what *A Course in Miracles* is about; expressed as such in numerous ways[6]. It is also what this book is about. This book is here to point you towards experiencing that in the beginning there was only Reality and in the end there will only be Reality.

Also, let us remind ourselves of the vitally important point regarding forgiveness: '*the key to forgiveness is to understand that thoughts of the ego are meaningless, as is the world of the Illusion*'[7]. In truth, neither exists. Forgiveness invites the Holy Spirit's correction, or chipping away at misperceptions, of the mind, ultimately leading you into full alignment with the thought process of the Holy Spirit; the experience of the non-existence of the Illusion.

Knowing all this is well and good, and it is important. A well understood framework within which to comprehend something is critical. And having a mental picture representing this in the form of the Reality Circle and the Illusion Circle can make it easier to cultivate this understanding. However, merely understanding it will not get you home.

Fortunately, you have been given tools to move you along your seeming journey in the Illusion. These tools have been provided to you by the Holy Spirit, your memory of your destination, your memory of your goal. In order to achieve your goal you need to use these tools.

The Holy Spirit is communicating with you in every way you are open to receive communication. Therefore, you are encouraged to be of an open mind. You can be communicated to in your dreams, via sentences that catch your attention, via written material, whether in a book, on the internet or elsewhere, via what people say, via how people behave and via nature, to mention some. And the most potent tool of all is to translate these communications into the proactive tool of forgiveness; forgiveness of Velcro thoughts or forgiveness of what you perceive as mental obstacles or resistances along your path. This is a very practical teaching. You can take, and are immensely helped along your journey by taking, proactive action through forgiveness.

Forgiveness is your primary job. Everything else is secondary. Everything else is the tapestry of life allowing events to take place that make the backdrops and the cues that become your forgiveness opportunities. So follow your guidance in everything you do, whether at work, in nature or your interactions with people in general. This is what will ultimately provide you with your forgiveness opportunities and give you the experiences that will encourage you to continue doing your forgiveness work.

When you experience resistance in your mind to the guidance of the Holy Spirit, apply the forgiveness process to this resistance, whether the resistance relates to being taken outside of your comfort zone, an interaction you have with a person, or another type of issue that causes a resistance or a Velcro experience. This issue can just have arisen or it could have arisen at some time in the past. It can even be a concern about the future. Irrespective of the time it pertains to, if it is causing a Velcro feeling, or emotional pain, or you have in any other way become guided to change your perception about it, you *will* benefit from applying the forgiveness process. Remind yourself that you can choose peace of mind instead of this, and your tool for achieving peace of mind is forgiveness.

In situations where I feel a resistance to forgive I often find the perspective of it not actually having happened[8] helpful. Reminding yourself that you are the main beneficiary of your forgiveness may be helpful too.

A summary of how a forgiveness opportunity arises is as follows:

⇨ You have bought into the ego story;
⇨ This has made a web of misperceptions in your mind;
⇨ These misperceptions give rise to mental attachments;
⇨ Mental attachments give rise to emotional pain;
⇨ The emotional pain is your reminder of a forgiveness opportunity;

Once reminded you perform the forgiveness process, and a part of your mind that gave rise to this emotional pain has now left your mind.

Through forgiveness, eventually all your misperceptions will be gone and your mind will be filled with the thoughts of the Holy Spirit only[9]. This by the way is something you cannot fail to achieve[10]. But your journey does not stop here. At this point you release the Illusion, including the Holy Spirit, and allow yourself to be embraced by Reality. As a very last step, you also need to let go of the *memory* of who you are in order to gain the *experience* of who you are.

Jesus achieved this in his lifetime. He completely forgave the world; in the latter parts of his life his mind was totally aligned with the thoughts and perceptions of the Holy Spirit.

You may or may not reach the goal of experiencing who you are in truth in this lifetime. But either way, since you are still reading this book the odds are that you are getting close to reaching this goal.

The above are the reminders for this teaching. When we first embark on learning something new, it often seems a major task; all these new ideas and concepts seem like a lot to get our head around. However, once we accomplish a task and look back at what we have learned it tends to look a lot more manageable than we thought it would be. If you were to read this book again, you may be surprised at how much easier you find digesting the information the second time around.

Well, this may very well be the beginning of your forgiveness practice. And at first it may seem a bit daunting to incorporate the mental discipline of forgiveness into your life. However, there is great power in taking that first small step. With a bit of willingness and with taking small steps, before you know it you will have built some nice momentum into your forgiveness practice. And the experiences you will have along the way will most likely result in you never choosing to look back.

Chapter 10

Final Thoughts

Remember, your goal is the goal. The means are never the goal. By focusing on staying mindful of your goal, the right means will always present themselves to you to keep you moving forward. Miracles may happen along the way. They are part of what will move you forward, but they are not the goal. Your goal is to experience yourself in truth.

Your most important tool in your tool box, by far, for reaching this goal is forgiveness. And you are already in the right place for your forgiveness opportunities to arise. If changes are due to happen in your life they will happen naturally. There is no need to force anything.

Through forgiveness your web of misperceptions is chipped away and through forgiveness your ability to communicate with the Holy Spirit is improved. It is through your forgiveness that you tap into love and peace as well as the power of the Holy Spirit. You become increasingly self-empowered through the Holy Spirit part of your mind as you move forward on your path.

And (i) forgiveness; (ii) putting the Holy Spirit in charge of your day; and (iii) doing one of the short meditations provided in Chapter 6, or a similar meditation of joining with the Holy Spirit, every morning and evening, is a very powerful mix for propelling you forward along your path.

As a general rule, first and foremost seek your own advice from the Holy Spirit, rather than asking others for advice. There are occasions though where you may struggle to connect with the advice the Holy Spirit has for you. In these instances the Holy Spirit will attempt to get through to you via a book, something you happen to hear, etc. And sometimes it will be via a person, as was the case with me when I met Fran.

From my meeting with Fran, as well as helping me to open up and become more receptive to information from the Holy Spirit in connection with this book, I was also left with some tangible clues about the book's content. For example, I have mentioned the dried out watering hole with all the dead fish. At one point on our journey through the canyons, we saw a big tarantula, which I understood to be a clue to use the term web of misperceptions in this book. Fran has this ability to connect with clues, often physical clues, which contain communication from the Holy Spirit. It was during our first walk, by Cathedral Rock, that Fran connected with the first physical clue. It was a small empty spirits' bottle, the type with content for one mixed drink.

Looking back at the spiritual books I have read in the past, I recall getting a lot out of for example *The Four Agreements* by Don Miguel Ruiz; which is compact while still conveying substantial, practical, deep and profound information.

I understood the small spirits' bottle Fran connected with and picked up near Cathedral Rock to be a message for me to keep the content of this spiritual book compact, yet potent enough to achieve its objective. This I have now done. I put the message into the small empty bottle. And I tossed it into the vastness of the ocean, not knowing where it would end up or who would pick it up. **You** found it, picked it up, opened it and read it. Thank you!

If the presented material resonates with you, stay focused on the goal. Get to experience yourself by gracefully uncovering your true self through forgiveness. Eventually, stand naked in readiness for Reality's embrace.

Index of References

Introduction
1. *A Course in Miracles* (ACIM), third ed.; Mill Valley, CA: Foundation for Inner Peace (2007).

Subsequent references to ACIM includes chapter, section, paragraph and sentence, where **T** is for *Text*, **W** is for *Workbook*, **M** is for *Manual for Teachers* and **C** is for *Clarification of Terms*.

Chapter 1 –Reality and Illusion
1. ACIM, T-14.III.4:4-5.
2. ACIM, T-12.IV.1:3-5.
3. ACIM, T-12.VIII.4:7.
4. ACIM, C-1.3:1.

Chapter 2 – It is All in the Mind
1. ACIM, T-1.VI.1:3.
2. ACIM, T-2.V.A.12(2):1.
3. ACIM, T-21.in.1:7.
4. ACIM, T-6.IV.2:9.
5. ACIM, T-7.III.3:2.
6. ACIM, T-7.III.3:4-5.
7. Renard, Gary R, *The Disappearance of the Universe: Straight Talk About Illusions, Past Lives, Religion, Sex, Politics, and the Miracles of Forgiveness*; Carlsbad, CA: Hay House, Inc (2004); p. 218.
8. ACIM, T-2.V.A.18.(8):2.
9. ACIM, T-1.VII.4:1.

Chapter 3 – There is No Form, Only Content
1. ACIM, T-4.II.8:1.
2. ACIM, T-4.II.8:8.

3. Renard, Gary R, *The Disappearance of the Universe: Straight Talk About Illusions, Past Lives, Religion, Sex, Politics, and the Miracles of Forgiveness*; Carlsbad, CA: Hay House, Inc (2004); pp. 142-143.
4. ACIM, W-16.
5. ACIM, T-21.in.1:1.
6. Renard, Gary R, *The Disappearance of the Universe: Straight Talk About Illusions, Past Lives, Religion, Sex, Politics, and the Miracles of Forgiveness*; Carlsbad, CA: Hay House, Inc (2004); pp. 159-160.
7. ACIM, T-31.VIII.3:1.
8. ACIM, T-20.VI.9:5-7.
9. ACIM, T-2.I.2:2.
10. ACIM, T-5.III.5:5.
11. ACIM, T-6.II.5:1-2.
12. ACIM, T-5.III.11:1-3.
13. ACIM, T-1.II.5:1.
14. ACIM, T-in.1:7.

Chapter 4 – There are No Coincidences
1. ACIM, W-132.6:2
2. ACIM, T-16.V.12:3.
3. ACIM, W-in.1:1.
4. ACIM, W-132.6:2.
5. ACIM, W-132.6:4-5.
6. ACIM, M-3.1.6.
7. ACIM, T.6.II.7:2-3.
8. *1984 Guinness Rekordbok*; 9th Norwegian ed, Chr. Schibsted Forlag (1983); p. 138.
9. Renard, Gary R, *Your Immortal Reality: How to Break the Cycle of Birth and Death*; Carlsbad, CA: Hay House, Inc (2006); p. 163(8).

Chapter 5 – There are Always Only Two Choices
1. ACIM, T-5.V.6:8.
2. ACIM, T-5.II.5:3.
3. ACIM, T-12.IV.1:3-5.
4. ACIM, T-1.I.36.
5. ACIM, T-5.II.7:1-4
6. ACIM, T-8.VIII.8:7.
7. ACIM, W-16.
8. ACIM, T-1.I.2:1.
9. ACIM, T-1.I.3:1.
10. ACIM, T-5.II.7:1-4.
11. ACIM, T-29.VII.1:1.
12. ACIM, W-32.2:1.
13. ACIM, W-347.
14. ACIM, T-17.I.2:4.

Chapter 7 – You are in Reality
1. ACIM, T-10.I.2:1.
2. ACIM, T-11.V.2:1-3.
3. ACIM, T-11.V.2:4.
4. ACIM, T-12.IV.6:1.

Chapter 8 – Remember Reality and Experience Yourself
1. ACIM, W-pII.1.1:3.
2. ACIM, W-46.1:1.
3. ACIM, T-1.VI.1:1.
4. ACIM, W-11.
5. Renard, Gary R, *The Disappearance of the Universe: Straight Talk About Illusions, Past Lives, Religion, Sex, Politics, and the Miracles of Forgiveness*; Carlsbad, CA: Hay House, Inc (2004); p. 253.
6. ACIM, W-34.
7. ACIM, T-31.III.1:4-5.
8. ACIM, M-8.6:1-2

9. Renard, Gary R, *The Disappearance of the Universe: Straight Talk About Illusions, Past Lives, Religion, Sex, Politics, and the Miracles of Forgiveness*; Carlsbad, CA: Hay House, Inc (2004); p. 255.
10. ACIM, W-pII.1.1:1.
11. Renard, Gary R, *The Disappearance of the Universe: Straight Talk About Illusions, Past Lives, Religion, Sex, Politics, and the Miracles of Forgiveness*; Carlsbad, CA: Hay House, Inc (2004); p. 218.
12. Renard, Gary R, *The Disappearance of the Universe: Straight Talk About Illusions, Past Lives, Religion, Sex, Politics, and the Miracles of Forgiveness*; Carlsbad, CA: Hay House, Inc (2004); p. 97.

Chapter 9 – Some Reminders

1. ACIM, T-2.I.2:2.
2. ACIM, T-5.II.5:3.
3. ACIM, T-20.VI.9:6-7
4. ACIM, T-5.III.10:1.
5. Renard, Gary R, *Your Immortal Reality: How to Break the Cycle of Birth and Death*; Carlsbad, CA: Hay House, Inc (2006); p. 164(18).
6. E.g. ACIM, T-3.VII.5:6, T-5.II.1:2, 3:8 and 4:4-5 and T-6.II.7:5-6 to mention some.
7. ACIM, W-11.
8. ACIM, W-pII.1.1:1.
9. ACIM, T-5.II.3:7-9.
10. ACIM, T-13.I.4:4-5.

Further Reading

If I were to recommend one book, in addition to *A Course in Miracles* itself, in order to assist and motivate you to stay focused on your goal, it is Gary R. Renard's *The Disappearance of the Universe*: Straight Talk about Illusions, Past Lives, Religion, Sex, Politics and the Miracles of Forgiveness. I cannot thank Gary enough for how helpful this book has been for me. Others have expressed similar gratitude.

One person who has expressed similar gratitude is Mike Lemieux. In response to his gratitude and in his wish to spread Gary Renard's message further, he wrote the book *Dude, Where's My Jesus Fish?*: A Compilation Highlighting the Blunt and Uncompromising Teachings of Arten And Pursah on *A Course in Miracles*. This book contains the highlights in a topic-based fashion from *The Disappearance of the Universe* as well as from Gary Renard's second book, *Your Immortal Reality*: How to Break the Cycle of Birth and Death. I also recommend this book.

It is often beneficial to read a book with real life examples of how someone else has gone about their forgiveness practice. For this, I recommend Susan Dugan's *Extraordinary Ordinary Forgiveness*.

It is also often beneficial to read the story of someone who has achieved the goal this book guides you toward; experiencing themselves in truth. For this, I recommend Carol M Howe's *Never Forget to Laugh*: Personal Recollections of Bill Thetford, Co-Scribe of *A Course in Miracles*.

About the Author

After leaving his work of more than ten years with an American bank in the City of London Karstein Bjastad became a stay-at-home dad.

Karstein had his spiritual interests re-kindled after leaving his career in the City of London. His spiritual quest led him to *A Course in Miracles*, which is a non-dualistic spiritual teaching.

The application of the teaching set out in *A Course in Miracles* has become Karstein's life passion, and one of his aims is to share his passion with others, largely through making available practical and easy-to-understand information about non-dualistic spirituality.

Karstein's website is www.karsteinbjastad.com

BOOKS

O is a symbol of the world, of oneness and unity. In different cultures it also means the "eye," symbolizing knowledge and insight. We aim to publish books that are accessible, constructive and that challenge accepted opinion, both that of academia and the "moral majority."

Our books are available in all good English language bookstores worldwide. If you don't see the book on the shelves ask the bookstore to order it for you, quoting the ISBN number and title. Alternatively you can order online (all major online retail sites carry our titles) or contact the distributor in the relevant country, listed on the copyright page.

See our website www.o-books.net for a full list of over 500 titles, growing by 100 a year.

And tune in to myspiritradio.com for our book review radio show, hosted by June-Elleni Laine, where you can listen to the authors discussing their books.

MySpiritRadio